How to Be a Supe

Living Life to the Max in you.

Dedication

Mandy, Pauline, Julie, and Mat,
young parents who died too soon

How to be
a
SuperAger

Living Life to the Max
in your 50s, 60s and beyond

Angela S Lucas

How to Be a SuperAger
Living Life to the Max in your 50s, 60s and beyond

First published in 2018 by
Panoma Press Ltd
48 St Vincent Drive, St Albans, Herts, AL1 5SJ UK

info@panomapress.com
www.panomapress.com

Cover design by Michael Inns
Artwork by Karen Gladwell
Original embroidery by Heidi Rhodes

ISBN 978-1-784521-36-3

This book is available online and in all good bookstores.

Testimonials

This book is truly inspirational and full of optimism, giving clear challenging advice for those struggling with the ageing process.

Paula Whittle BEd (Hons) MA MBA FRSA,
Education and Leadership Consultant

This inspirational practical book is a delight for those over 50 who feel their life adventure is over when in fact it has not yet begun.

Elva Ainsworth FCIPD,
Author and Business Leader

Acknowledgements

Mindy Gibbins-Klein – *www.bookmidwife.com* –
without whom this book would not have
been possible.

Elva Ainsworth – who first saw the potential for this
book to be written.

Kevin Lucas – Encourager ++ and creator of my
website and setting up all the social media.

The reviewers who kindly gave their time, in
particular **Paula Whittle** who went above and beyond
the requirements of a reviewer.

Contents

Introduction

Why did I write this book and indeed, what qualifies me to write it? If you met me you would shake hands with a very ordinary 83-year-old mother to 5 adult children and 11 grandchildren. In the everydayness of my life this family is my real achievement; when they are around I go into matriarchal mode and reflect that if I didn't exist then neither would they. There is something about the achievements of their lives that extends the meaning and purpose of my life, taking my beginnings into their future.

So, is that it? Not at all. There was a trigger that moved me into a journey that, while inevitably marked 'getting older', also opened up new thought patterns.

Becoming aware of such privilege began in my late midlife. Shockingly and unexpectedly, a friend of my adult children died. Her untimely death was soon followed by that of other young parents. Each of them would have loved my opportunity to get older, to go to university as a mature student, to learn new skills that would take me to work in the Middle East, and to write this book. It would be so disrespectful to waste my opportunities, don't you think?

This book's dedication is to those young parents: to Julie, mother of five young children; to Mandy, mother of two toddlers, one of whom died with her in a tragic accident. Then there is Pauline, mother to three daughters, and Mat, my son-in-law and father to three older teenagers.

To celebrate my 82nd birthday, with my daughter, I hiked the final 100 kilometres (62 miles) of the ancient pilgrimage route the Camino de Santiago de Compostela in the Galician mountains of Spain and, in doing so, learned a lot about myself. The Camino reflected much of the adventure of becoming not only a third ager but also the experience of entering new territory as a SuperAger.

And new territory it certainly is with parameters not only set by health, finances and personal circumstances, but also very largely by the way this strange land of getting older can be perceived.

My mother lived to the age of 103; her mother also lived to a great age. If longevity is in my genetic makeup then the coming years just have to be filled with purpose, with something that gives meaning to the privilege of being alive.

My hope is that as you read this book you will be captivated by the possibilities coming your way. Your life is unlikely to be as smooth as the still lake in the local park, at least not all of the time. There will often be times when life is like the devastating floods that pour into people's homes destroying everything material built up over the years. But if you are reading this you are alive. So don't dream your life, live your dreams and become that exceptional person that only you can be.

Don't Dream Your Life   **Live Your Dreams**

Ageing is Inevitable   **Stagnation is Optional**

Angela Lucas

CHAPTER ONE

Life is a gift, use it well

Enjoy life, it has an expiry date

Your life is a precious and wonderful thing; you can't just sit down and let it lap around you, you have to plunge into it, you have to dive through it. You can't save it or store it up, you can't hoard it in a vault. You have to taste it, you have to use it. The more you use the more you have and that is the miracle of it.

These are not my words, I read them some time some place and stored them in my memory, but the truth remains that you get to live this life on planet Earth once and it is almost disrespectful to waste that honoured gift.

Live while you are alive, remembering that this moment in time is a gift, so don't wistfully dream your life, live your dreams. If you are reading this book then hopefully you have been drawn by the title and noted the strapline which hopefully has appeal for third agers, a grouping facing some difficult questions. What has life been all about? What will my legacy be? How do I live a fulfilling life? Of course, these questions could be relevant to any person of any age and perhaps the earlier addressed so the more useful.

Third agers are usually defined as people probably of retirement age, with reasonable health, although that is not a necessity, and usually between the ages of 50 to 70 but can push well into older age. Now aged 83 I still include myself in that bracket although I long abandoned the term Autumn Gold.

To celebrate my 82nd birthday, my daughter and I chose to walk the final 100 kilometres (62 miles) of an ancient pilgrimage route in northern Spain, this was the Camino de Santiago de Compostela, but more about that adventure later. Sufficient to say at this point is that as we walked, challenged by mud, deep sticky mud, steep terrain, and 30 degree heat, I realised how much the pilgrimage mirrored many of the challenges faced by those at the third age stage of life. However, if you are younger or older than this stage, do read on, you will probably find it relevant. While my Camino adventure was at a post-midlife time, my own get up and go got moving in my 60s.

The Camino challenges are physical, emotional and spiritual, but it is reasonable to repeat here that the lessons learned along the route mirrored much of the lessons learned along the way in life's journey. You walk, work, sleep and eat – the necessities of daily life. But behind the scenes there is much more happening. Already you know that it is the difficulties you have encountered which have proved to be a toughening-up experience; these experiences helped to shape your character, to make you into the person you are today. And now, with reflection, you realise that life has had all the components of an amazing adventure. While adventures have good bits, fun bits and exciting bits, it is in the very nature of an adventure that it also has worrying times, scary and unnerving times, anxious nail-biting times, but you have survived regardless of the obstacles. Helen Keller, a lady born deaf and blind, once commented that to let life leak out, to let it wear away by the mere passage of time, or to withhold giving it and spreading it is to choose nothing.

To be a third ager is to enter new territory; this is a country you have not been to before although you may have observed it in the life of other people, of parents, older friends and neighbours. This is a time when the landscape of your own familiar territory has been removed and your life is taking on a different shape that needs exploring. Remember that adventures include the worrying moments and part of your exploration will include concerns about getting older. But, of course, getting older is exactly what you have been doing since the time you were born and it has not been a deterrent to living.

The Black American author, activist and wise woman, Maya Angelou, has described this time in life as being plump with promise, but what does that mean? You will have noticed that many of your peer group have poor health or limited finances while others you see seem to go on endless cruises and exotic holidays. But this is about you, the territory that is yours to claim and inhabit.

For sure your dreams may be bounded by difficult personal circumstances; however, you do have some say in how they work out. Give some thought to what you can control and what you can't. For example, you schedule a hot air balloon ride but you have no control over the weather, so, by default, you have no control about if and when the ride will happen. There are some things that you do have control over: you can choose not to be defeated if the ride doesn't happen; you can still choose some other things – what to eat that day, whether to exercise or to refrain from smoking. You can even choose to rebook the balloon ride.

While this is possibly a time to chart a new course, it isn't necessary to know exactly how your ideal life will take shape. At this stage you only need to know what feels better and what feels worse and then to work with that raw material. There is no need for everything to be in place, it is only necessary to make a start, to metaphorically put one foot in front of the other to start making progress.

Remember again that adventures have obstacles and at times your dreams may even be birthed in difficulty and seem impossible. This is the time to allow yourself to imagine your dream as a reality and take some steps to overcome the difficulty. J K Rowling, the *Harry Potter* author, with nowhere else suitable as a place to write, spent her days in a café with her notepads and just began to craft her books.

Sometimes it is in the most difficult of times that you will see your dream stand out and you begin to reimagine the possibility. There is a simple truth: you can stick a candle into a dark place and it will continue to shine. A friend reminded me that there is another old saying: A closed door emits no light.

It is a truism that the older you get the faster time seems to fly by and one day it will seem as if tomorrow is yesterday, Your life on planet Earth will only happen once; today will never come back, so if at all possible, savour and feel the moment even if your thoughts are running down the road and you have to chase after them to bring them back to the present moment.

Your thoughts might have contained regrets, but even these may have a purpose and become manageable if given an opportunity to address them. My relationship with my mother had always been poor and, although she lived in Australia, as the years went by it became increasingly important for me to do bridge building. At about five-yearly intervals I was able to travel out to visit her. At first those visits, clouded by acrimony, left me feeling it would have been wiser not to have bothered. However, once dementia became my mother's alter ego she no longer saw me as her daughter of bygone years but rather as someone new entering her life, someone she was more at ease with. The dementia also served as a barrier between me and the past, allowing for a gentler approach, until one day I realised that almost without my noticing, a measure of warmth and affection for her had crept in and I could only be sad for the bitterness of her life. The regrets dealt with, when my mother died aged 103 there was just gratitude for the opportunities to make something better out of a difficult past.

Your regrets will be different yet nonetheless it is observable that most regrets involve some form of relationship breakdown: the relationship between parent and child, between friends, and too often due to the breakdown of marriage. Even so, wherever possible it is worth making the effort to live peaceably with others as far as circumstances and personal temperament permit. You alone are privy to the deepest regrets that you own and so it is you alone who can know how to dismantle them and not allow them to disable this precious late midlife time.

Whatever your circumstances, do not allow yourself to drift into dreaming your life away and thus adding it to the list of regrets later in life. You alone have the choice to live passively or actively, and of course, and very understandably, you may feel that this is a time in life when you have earned the right to wind down with a little folding of the hands and resting of the feet.

Your work life might have been tough and unrewarding, it may have been boring or back-breaking, only for you to find that the demands of home life left little space or time to explore hobbies, never mind to explore the wider world. You may be one of many who has always lived right where you do now, perhaps in Essex, Lancashire or Scotland, and you may be content to continue to do so. You could be shouting at this printed page with frustration and indignation at the talk of adventure because your lifestyle is limited by health problems, poverty and a caring role. Even so, you still have the potential to develop and to broaden the parameters of your life. You are not defined by your health or your wealth but rather by the deeply natural, essential and intrinsic person only you can be. There is not and never can be another you anywhere.

When my daughter and I hiked in the Galician mountain range of northern Spain for two weeks we carried all we needed in rucksacks, walking about 10 miles a day, we slept in dormitories and used communal shower space. A daily need was to find somewhere to eat that provided eggs, some protein, with the toast for breakfast rather than just marmalade. Along the trail there also seemed to be a dearth of fruit or vegetables. We had left behind at home the demands of the washing machine and the washing-up, even the joyless BBC with dreadful news of worldwide atrocities and terrorism. Our minds were freed up to explore not only new geographical locations but also to discover that we were companions on a steep road, meeting other pilgrims, walking alongside them sometimes for a short while and listening to the life stories of others.

We met people who were walking with advanced cancer, with broken bones and with broken hearts, yet who had the urgency and will to find a deeper purpose to life. I, like many of those other pilgrims, was completely out of my comfort zone. The territory we explored was not only the mountains and the early morning mist of the forests, but was also an inner journey of discovery about myself, about my strengths and weaknesses, and I came to the realisation that it was possible to go beyond myself. Until I gave it a go I never knew that I could do it.

Already you know that not too many people get through life without experiencing the downsides of life alongside the positive experiences, and you will have noticed that it is the tough times which produce an enduring spirit.

You can never live long enough to experience the fullness of all that life can offer, so make the most of your now opportunity while making the most of the possibility to live your dreams. Are you thinking that given your circumstances this is not going to happen? Think of

Stephen Hawking, the amazing, talented scientist who, totally paralysed by motor neurone disease, still scans space to explore its mysteries. His body restrictions haven't tethered his mind or imagination. Currently the only movement he is able to make is the twitch of a muscle in his cheek; this miniscule twitch is used to control a computer allowing him to engage with other scientists and mathematicians to explore vast worlds beyond our own.

Allow yourself to draw on your past life experiences, including its sorrows and disappointments, utilising both good and bad to enhance the possibility of benefiting today and all of your tomorrows.

In the next chapter we can explore your active legacy. Intrigued? Read on.

CHAPTER TWO

An active legacy

The measure of a life is not its duration
but its donation.

~ Rev. Peter Marshall

So what has it all been about, the striving, the learning, the working, the nurturing, the tough times? I quote Oprah Winfrey who asserts that what she knows for sure is this: you are built not to shrink down to less but to blossom into more, to be more splendid, to be more extraordinary.

Now here is a thought: did you know that something of the uniqueness of the person you have grown to be can also be part of the future even when you are no longer here? In the final chapter I present some ideas for you to consider that will help to answer that question. Intrigued? Just read on.

If you have a living faith, prayer is a means of securing your legacy, even if that is not the immediate intention. One day, feeling rather sad that I will not be around to meet my grandchildren's children, it dawned on me that though I may not be able to hold them in my arms in this life, I can hold them in my heart now in prayer and be a blessing for their future.

But of course, a personal faith in the Living God isn't all about pie in the sky, it is also about jam on your bread today. Being a blessing in prayer might seem a bit far-fetched to some, but a measure of encouragement to someone living now can also be called a blessing.

It can't be emphasised often enough that to be alive is a privilege. For you to get to this age is a privilege, too many people have died too young. A major motivating factor for me has been the sad and sometimes traumatic death of my adult children's friends – fine young people who would have loved my opportunity to grow old, to be a third ager and beyond, to just be alive. It would be almost disrespectful not to live life to the fullest extent possible, to go beyond disappointments and disadvantages, and truly be alive rather than wistfully dreaming as time goes by.

Every day above ground is a good one. Every new morning is a promise of hope for you to grasp. Midlife is not a watershed for permission to start going downhill. Hopefully your midlife is a time to stop and assess your journey, to consider how or where you go from this point in time. Boredom is bad for your health while the act of breathing alone gives your brain a dose of endorphins to enhance your health and sense of wellbeing.

That there are advantages to being proactive in your midlife years is recognised by the University of the Third Age where it has been shown that to belong to a likeminded group, using your brain, and keeping your mind supple and active helps to delay the onset of dementia. There is something about being proactive that helps to release needful hormones. You can take an interest alongside others in the history of our country. You can explore the vastness of space or learn a new language. You can learn to play the recorder, the piano, and in some areas, even learn to play the harp. You can contribute to a group passing on your own wealth of knowledge.

Are you still in need of motivation? Google *'Growing Old Disgracefully'*. I'll tantalise you with the thought and leave you to discover the joyous zaniness of people who are living while they are alive. However, in the final chapter there will be some more information.

Know this for sure that whatever your life has been up to this moment in time, it is not necessary to settle for just more of the same, unless of course that is what you want to do. Your life has endowed you with enough material to enhance the life of at least one other person. I enjoyed this quote which was heard in passing so am passing it on to you: 'Time is a dressmaker specialising in alterations!'

Over the years your priorities will have changed as you passed through the many stages of life. Your work life may have come to an end, if you had children they may have flown the proverbial nest, you may be a carer for an elderly relative, but whatever your circumstances you want to be someone who counts, to do something that counts, to be more than the shadow dodging your footsteps. Whatever the legacy you will leave, of this one thing you can be sure: the best legacy is one that leaves things tidy, and the kindest component is to do with relationships.

Some years ago I worked as a Marie Curie nurse; that is, someone who is involved in the final few days of a terminally ill cancer patient and in their own home while supporting not only the patient but also the family. Not once did I hear someone regret not having a bigger house, or going on cruises, or seeing the Northern Lights. Those who rested easily in their final days were those who had nurtured relationships. A poignant poem by Linda Ellis tells it well. *The Dash* refers to the dash between the date you were born and the date that you die.

> *For it is not how much we own*
> *The cars, the house, the cash*
> *What matters is how we live and love*
> *And how we spend our dash*

The choices you make now are so different from those of your earlier years and will most likely have different values. Perhaps it is time to own who you are now rather than the image projected on to you by others. To live your dreams may take courage and hard work to make them happen, but consider that may be better than years later regretting not having done so.

You can be your own hero by embracing the possibility of change. Sometimes change is forced on you and is inevitable because of circumstances, yet these inevitable circumstances may be the very times when you find that you are capable of so much more, and usually when you least expect to do so.

Sometimes it is helpful to speak your dreams out loud and thereby making them a commitment or a plan. When I rather daringly announced my Camino plans the response was somewhat overwhelmingly negative. Comments ranged from concerns about my ability to walk for 10 miles on one day, never mind for 14 consecutive days, to concerns about what if I fell and broke something? Well, I did fall and damaged both my hip and my dignity but picked myself up and carried on. There were those who thought I was being irresponsible and might die in the mountains, and of course that could be true, but equally I could die of boredom sitting in front of the television. Perhaps this is the space to explain that we were not climbing mountains as do those with ropes up craggy Mount Everest; not at all, we were following trails in the Galician mountain range, trails that led through forests, through mud, rocky passes, more mud, actually lots of mud, and also some beautiful wide open spaces.

Nonetheless, once the decision was made and spoken out loud it meant that, regardless of the risks, I believed in the possibility of a tomorrow where I could live out my dream.

Somewhat late in life, in my 60s and reflecting that I had only ever been average at anything, it seemed time to at least get one A Level. So I enrolled at the local college to study English Literature. Being in a class of young people was rejuvenating. The mid-morning coffee breaks became opportunities to hear about the lives of the young students who were growing up in a world vastly different from the one we knew as young people. With hindsight I can see that particular journey was the beginning of helping me to understand the importance of carving out for myself a place in the lives of the present young generation, but again, there will be more about this in a later chapter.

You may never have any desire either to go to college or to walk part of the ancient Camino route, but whatever your chosen path there will be things in common. Already you will have noted that to get to this point in time you have been on your own life journey. You may have had to change your mindset many times as different challenges arose. You may have had to go beyond the possibilities that you thought you were capable of and discovered new depths and strengths as you learned to discard your weaknesses.

My Camino challenges resulted in some useful weight loss and some firming up of previously unused muscles. I developed a sense of wellbeing in the discovery of personal insights, not just physical but also emotional and spiritual.

As an inhabitant of planet Earth, encourage yourself to be as physically active as your health permits; just considering the personal advantages can be a great motivator. Ask around, do some research and you will find so many examples of people who have lived their lives more fully by turning their dreams into a valid reality.

For me, and really close to home, was the example of a family member who, in her 60s, completed a degree with the Open University and finally did a PhD in psychology. An example further removed is that of Stephen Hawking whose life story was made into a film in 2016. If ever you doubt your own possibilities, watch the film and be inspired. A few years ago I heard the remarkable story of a lady who was born multi-handicapped, and then became blind as a young teenager; obviously she was totally dependent on others for her physical needs. As a young woman she studied to become a counsellor, in late midlife she married. This remarkable woman speaks on BBC radio, addresses audiences to encourage and motivate, and in recent years set up a charity to provide accommodation for profoundly handicapped people and their carers or families.

Be aware, stuff happens and your dreams may seem to be railroaded. Here, and with permission, I recount the difficulties and eventual successes of one woman who refused to bury her dream.

'I lost my job, had a breakdown and my brother suggested that I went back into studying. So I decided to go back and do it while I worked for myself. I am not very good at doing nothing and so this was something to do during the quiet times. I also had applied for a few jobs and was turned down because I didn't have an MSc. Even though I had reached a very senior level and been in business for thirty years. It was also like everyone else thought I was too old. In my head age is really irrelevant, but this is not quite true. Studying is much harder when you are older, less new brain to absorb things or something. I struggled to remember things. Mum has Alzheimer's so I was worried about that and thought this would be a good way to stay mentally active. I started this Master's 19 years ago but dropped out when my dad died during my exams. I went back to university two years ago, so you can imagine that for me to graduate now is a big deal.'

Her personal story of triumph despite tragedy is awesome, don't you think?

Using your activity well is an asset to help in managing mental health. Just as man, or woman, cannot live without dreams so they cannot live well without hope. Hope epitomises the future. Here is an example of hope in action: did you know that to plant seeds in the garden is to believe there is a tomorrow for the seeds to flourish?

CHAPTER THREE

Time to celebrate and get motivated

Stand up to your obstacles, you will find that they do not have the strength you think they have.

~ Norman Vincent Peale

Not everyone gets the opportunity to grow older so savour the moment, use your gift wisely and well; hopefully you have already discovered that attitude of mind plays a major part in contributing to the planning of these special years.

Maybe you shuddered when, on your 60th birthday, the offers for funeral plans started to drop through your letterbox. *Plan Your Funeral Now And Get £50 Off.* I remember thinking it would be more helpful to give me the £50 at the time rather than for someone else to have the amount debited off my funeral bill. On the other hand, some other useful offers are available as you become eligible for the blessings of free prescriptions, bus passes and offers of bowel screening!

Further blessings become evident as a new kind of beauty emerges; the mystery is that the beauty of a young person's face moves to the heart, while conversely the beauty of the heart is reflected in the beauty of the face. Think of the actresses Dame Helen Mirren and Dame Judi Dench who have earned the facial fine line wrinkles which portray the essence of their lives, both personal and professional.

Yet do not be fooled into thinking that this is a time to chill and not bother to take care of yourself; you can be the SuperAger who defies the notion that midlife is the time to start a journey towards becoming a virtual geriatric. It isn't about having enough money in the bank but rather is about the attitude residing in your heart. You may have developed the shape of a bumble bee, regard it is a badge of honour because you have lived long enough to acquire it. Nonetheless do be aware that your shape, whether that of a bumble bee, a tall thin stick insect or whatever other adjective you wish to choose, is not an excuse to indulge in cosy slippers and baggy cardigans, not unless that is a choice consciously made. You have the privilege of reaching this age, so celebrate. Every day above ground is an opportunity and a treat, so make the most of it.

It is rarely too late to become what you might have been as you bring the years of experience and maturity into your plans. The mantra remains true that age is more than just a number; it has value incorporating experience, maturity and wisdom. Lucky you if you are among those who have more time once retired because many retirees are so busy they wonder how they managed to find the time to go to work.

As you explore this new territory allow yourself to chart a new course. Too often life just seems to happen without your permission; however, there are also times that you can make life happen. This may be the opportunity to reinvent yourself – remember that it is rarely too late to become what you might have been. Try this for size: make a collage of your aspirations, stick it on a prominent wall adding to it as fresh ideas come to mind.

In the previous chapter I wrote of coming to education rather late in life. But that wasn't my journey alone. In her autobiography, round the world lone yachtswoman Ellen MacArthur tells the gripping story of her nerve-shredding, nail-biting adventure as she sailed solo around the world. Her seemingly impossible voyage was captured on camera and relayed around the world via television screens. At the age of 28 she had become the fastest person to sail solo around the world and says she got her single-mindedness from her grandmother, who at the age of 80 graduated with her degree in English. Just how Ellen MacArthur, this tiny young woman, manoeuvred her yacht through roaring seas, and in mega gale-force winds climbed the mast to do necessary repairs, is beyond the imagination of most of us. Where did her sheer gutsy inspiration come from you might wonder? While her parents and precious

Aunt Thea were always very supportive, it was her grandmother who bequeathed the gifts of grit and determination which inspired her granddaughter.

This very ordinary, yet extraordinary, grandma was brought up in poverty and, like many of her generation, had little formal education. In her 60s she decided to remedy that omission and went back to school, often joining in with the local schoolchildren to do basic subjects. She persevered so well that eventually going to college became the next step. College gave way to university where she was 'The Old' in a class of young people. Halfway through her final year she was diagnosed with cancer. Not one to give up and encouraged by her university community, she completed her degree although sadly dying a few months later. At her graduation she received a standing ovation from her fellow students. How deeply proud she would have been of her granddaughter's determination to succeed.

My proudest accolade is a mention in the acknowledgements of my granddaughter's PhD. She wrote that she was inspired by both her Granny and Grandma who came to academic education late in life. Her beloved Granny, late in life, had also gained her PhD. I am the Grandma who did not get a PhD but did write this book.

It is rarely too late to reinvent yourself and in doing so to enrich your own life while encouraging that of others around you. Ageing actively is positive for you and is also an encouragement for those coming along behind you. Remember that every day is a gift. You may just hate waking up and tumbling out of bed, perhaps contemplating a boring day at work or a basket full of washing to be put in the machine, but it just has to be better than waking up and finding you are dead, to have died in your sleep!

This is a reflective time and you may be wondering what it, life, has all been about and also what your life legacy will be. If your thoughts are negative explore the possibility to do something about your life and your living while there is still time. It helps to get goal orientated; consider that planting bulbs in the chill of autumn speaks of springtime tomorrow. Learning a new skill or having an adventure, doing something positive outside your usual parameters can breathe fresh oxygen and vitality into the mundane and make you feel good about yourself.

There can be many motivating reasons to get you out of bed and, having indulged in coffee and croissants, to get you moving. My friend's husband, now in his late 70s, works alongside the English teacher at the local college. His presence and experience are an encouragement for the class tutor and skill enhancing for the young students.

I have goals, some are maybe unrealistic, but nonetheless they are motivating. In another chapter you will read about the goal setting and practical preparation to hike along part of the ancient Camino de Santiago, but here I will let you into my aspirations. I aspire to abseil, to ski, to go rock climbing and, somewhat hopefully and very improbably, go to the weddings of my great-grandchildren who, as yet, are unborn. It is good to have a dream and to work towards living your dream. Not that I can do anything about those great-grandchildren.

It is good to have a reason to get out of bed in the morning. Martin Luther King famously announced, 'I have a dream today' and he worked towards making it a reality. Assassination cut his life short but he had set a standard which others were quick to pick up and aim to turn into reality. Martin Luther King didn't dream his life; while he was alive he not only lived his dream but became a standard for future generations who, becoming acquainted with his courageous story, resolved to live their own dreams.

Focus on what you can do rather than on what you can't do. This is time again just now to remember Professor Stephen Hawking who explores the extremities of space while totally immobilised by motor neurone disease. The man is living beyond anything that most of us can imagine. Think about your life legacy, think about the life-enhancing gifts you can bequeath to your friends or family, or even to your wider community. It is worth repeating that it is rarely too late to become what you want to be. It is rarely too late to do some form of training. Adventuring around the world might not be what you have in mind, but you already have gifts. Yours might be that of an encourager, a person of prayer, or someone who has the natural ability to impart enthusiasm; if so you may want to consider doing something about enhancing all or some of those abilities. And do remember that not everything requires great effort, skill or money.

A life lesson I learned in my early 70s, and would love to share with you, was to deliberately set out to do something to bless, enhance or encourage the day of someone else. No training required, no money involved, at least not unless you wish to invest a little. All that is needed is some get up and go and a willing heart.

One cold and drizzly winter's day, feeling defeated and deflated and unable to shake off the mood of being useless, I had a chat with God (you could call it prayer). I didn't ask for lots of money or a clever brain but for some oomph – that difficult to describe stuff that puts some oil in the engine of life. You may have other ways to motivate yourself, but nonetheless a thought came into my head, it was to go out of the house and positively do something to make three people feel good about themselves.

Going out in the miserable weather wasn't quite what I had in mind; still, I set off and walked for about two miles to a large supermarket complex. Once there and panicking, I thought, now what do I do? The nearest person to me was at the customer service desk and she became my target for opportunity. But again, what could I do? Then I noticed her fingernails which were vibrantly coloured, the startling red was sprinkled with flecks of gold. The woman smiled as I admired the handiwork, commenting on the vibrancy of colour on such a dull day. Briefly she told me about the young Chinese man at her local nail parlour who did her nails every fortnight. Her enthusiasm gathered pace as she talked of the young man's family, of his hopes and dreams for their future when he wanted to own his own nail bar instead of working for someone else.

After that it was much easier to approach other people and to offer compliments. There was an elegant lady who had her snow-white hair tipped with fine purple. A man on the shop floor was carefully arranging a display of apples. How normal it felt, how easy to make those compliments, to hopefully make someone else's day. I came home walking tall instead of slouching and felt invigorated to handle the rest of the day. You may struggle to believe this bit, but on the way home I met Father Christmas – yes, truly, but that story will have to wait for another book.

While focusing on what you can do rather than on what you can't do, you might want to consider some preparation. For my supermarket trip of encouragement all I needed to do was make the effort to get up and move. The Camino preparations were much more involved. For example, there will be some necessary preparations if you are thinking of volunteer opportunities as you will need to get a DBS police check – time consuming but necessary. Check out your local college to find out if you can pursue your hobby there and, if so, what preparations might be needed before a course begins. Perhaps photography is your choice; if so, does the course require you to buy any special equipment beforehand?

Your preparations can, and probably should, include freeing up space in your mind. Debilitating concerns about healthcare and finances can be addressed by taking some practical steps. You may already have written your Will; if not, then perhaps this is the time to do it. This isn't about focusing on your death but simply informing others of your wishes so that you are free to get on with living. Make sure that your Will is lodged where it will be easily found when required of course. The same applies to making a Power of Attorney; if possible, and with the help of a solicitor, make arrangements for positive action concerning your future health and finances to be taken care of. Then having done so, to inform whoever among your family or friends needs to know, put the documents in a safe place and get on with living.

Anxieties about the possibility of deteriorating future health can in part be mitigated by writing a Living

Will. In your own words you are able to set out your wishes about end of life treatment. My Living Will states simply that I do not wish extreme measures to be taken to prolong my life in the event of extreme illness or in the event of a totally debilitating accident. You can address and release some of those concerns; no solicitor is needed unless you are writing a complicated document. Just get your signature witnessed and lodge copies of the letter with those who may need them, including your GP, and then get on with living.

So, what is your motivation for some life-enhancing living? Largely I have been motivated to live my life to its fullest possible extent by the early deaths of some of my children's friends and, more recently, the death of my precious son-in-law. The far too early deaths of these young people made me very aware of the privilege I have had to get older, to have grandchildren, to study and to travel. Those young people would have loved my opportunities and it would be disrespectful to live my life aimlessly when their opportunities were cut short. To waste my life would be dishonouring.

Your motivating factors will be different; meanwhile, however, keeping yourself informed about issues – local, family or worldwide – will help to keep your mind alert. It is possible that while you follow your own ambitions you may also be able to use your lifetime experiences to be an encourager; there are so many ways this can be done. For instance, just for a start, you can volunteer to help out in a local enterprise, or you can go further and explore working with an organisation such as VSO, Voluntary Service Overseas, which utilises the experiences and skills of retired people to benefit overseas projects. There will be more VSO information in the final chapter of this book. Remember that ageing is inevitable but stagnation doesn't have to be.

CHAPTER FOUR

Go beyond the possible

Anyone who stops learning is old,
whether at twenty or eighty.

~ Henry Ford

Now that you have decluttered your mind you can dare yourself to think bigger, wiser and more courageously than before. This isn't a time to settle for normal, it's time to make a plan, to develop a spirit of adventure and curiosity, to show up and be your own hero.

As you encourage yourself to go for your dreams, a word of caution: it is wise to be just a little realistic, acknowledging that your dreams will only come to fruition as you work towards making them so. Wishful thinking won't achieve anything beyond regrets. It will be your mindset that helps you to create the change that allows you to go beyond yourself and live out the challenges to become the person that you dare to be. Be a risk taker – that is so much better than to find yourself cubbyholed into boredom or inactivity. Go beyond the possible to find the joy of having lived. Perhaps this bit of advice might help you: think back to a time in life when you felt well, energetic, etc. then allow yourself to behave as if you were that age. It takes practice but is very worthwhile and helps to re-energise your whole way of thinking. It's not, **if** I can, but **when** I can.

My 50s were that kind of time for me, a positive time when I learned to ride a horse, and to fall off. I went to college full-time for two years to gain a qualification which later enabled me to work in Saudi Arabia as a medical secretary. This was followed by time in Egypt teaching English at The British Council while also learning Arabic. Now, when everything feels like too much effort, I imagine myself at 50 years old, and discover that in short bursts it works, giving me just the push needed for the moment.

This is a good point to just pause and reflect about your journey to this moment. There comes a time when you have fulfilled all of life's markers. You were born and went through all the phases of toddlerhood and, emerging with a hint of your developing personality, this little human being started to make a mark on the world. All too soon you started going to school and I am guessing that your school days were rather different from those of a five-year-old starting school today. Do you remember the mid-morning bottle of milk, lukewarm from being in the sun too long? And horror of horrors, there was the nit nurse, we called ours Nitty Nora.

Back then the streets were safer and it is likely you were one of the little ones allowed to walk to school alone, or at least without an adult. My first day at school stands sharp in my memory. My father had walked me to the school gates, handed me a packet of jam sandwiches and said he would be back to collect me at the end of the school day. But when midday arrived I tearfully ran all the way back home. Why? Because the teacher told me off for not having a toothbrush.

School days were surely different. And at this point I have to mention that this is the only bit of reflective dreaming permissible! Perhaps you remember playing skipping while reciting a rhyme? We used to skip to the jingle *'Nebuchadnezzar the king of the Jews, bought his wife a pair of shoes...'* Or, if there were no teachers around we skipped to *'I saw me Aunty Clara sitting on the bumdelera...!'*

And oh the fun of hopscotch, where you played a jumping counting game and the girls usually outplayed the boys, who preferred marbles. Yet, even so, how envying it was to see another child's vibrant blue marble where deep blues were cut across with stabs of creamy white and deep magenta. It may be that even now you still retain some of the friendships formed in those early days. As an army family we were often on the move so friendships were unlikely to survive. My daughter, now in her 50s, regularly visits the friend she made when they were five years old, which of course means that now she is eligible to read this book – because, Wehay! She is a third ager. In fact all of my five children are third agers... hmmm... they might just get this book for Christmas!

I wonder which path your life took on leaving school. Many of your contemporaries went straight into office work while learning shorthand and typing. Others were fortunate enough to gain an apprenticeship which, back then, almost guaranteed a job for life. Now school leavers no longer have that promise of permanent and settled employment, how difficult it is for them to understand your world. A world where the nearest telephone was in a red box nowhere near to your home. A world when you stayed in touch with your friends by writing letters.

Another of life's markers has to be the whole boyfriend/ girlfriend scenario. Back then speed dating hadn't been invented, internet dating was unheard of. People got to know each other at work, watching football, over a drink in the pub or in the church youth club. The slower pace was a rite of passage that could lead to marriage.

If so, then more stages followed and possibly included babies, nappies, exasperating teenagers and acne until somehow those longed-for children disappeared to forge their own lives, leaving behind the empty nest syndrome. A raw and grieving time for sure, but also the beginning of something new for you. Of course your own raw and grieving time might be for the nest that never happened and you could almost think with envy the thought of fledglings flying away. This is a time to stir up your flagging energies to explore a wider world. I wish you well if you are able to take some tentative steps towards becoming a fulfilled SuperAger.

One day when I expressed exasperation about the current persistent attachment to mobile phones, I was wisely chided by my younger daughter that I needed to understand the world of those mobile-hugging young people and realise that they could not inhabit my world because so much has changed. In this climate of instant communication, instant coffee and instant gratification you can buy your fruit already peeled. No matter the nostalgia for the familiar world of not only your youth but also of last week, the reality is that life has forever changed. But nostalgia put aside, you can play catch up and involve yourself in so much more that this new world has to offer.

Your work world may have promised stability rather than excitement; your wages may have been low but were assured. Perhaps you find today's world too fast, too instant, too unstable, yet it is this very world which offers you the opportunities to engage with so much more. You can go to college, even to university, and get that long-coveted degree. Finances and health permitting, you can learn to ski, to rock climb, to paint, to stretch your imagination. You can explore this strange new world, you can go beyond the assumed possibilities, and in doing so discover a remarkable new you. Happy adventuring!

Are you reading this and thinking that I don't understand you are living on the breadline, either because of low wages or getting by on a state pension? I do understand because I have been in that horrible position. When first on my own with just my youngest child still at home, I didn't have a bank account with back-up money to pay the rent or the utility bills and was almost at the point of being evicted from my council house because of rent arrears. 'Almost' meant at four o'clock on a particular day. That I wasn't evicted and managed somehow to claw myself to some kind of stability is a story for another book. But I mention this to assure you that I write to you from a heart that has been shaped over the years by holding on to my dreams and finding ways to make them a reality.

As already mentioned, my own third age explorations began in my 50s and 60s. After working in the Middle East I went to evening classes to get an A Level in English Literature and, while sitting in the classroom watching the young students fill in their university application forms, such an amazing thought pinged into my brain. Do you know what, I could do that. Quickly I went to the college office and amused the secretary by asking for my own university application form, and my next adventure had begun. There was the nail-biting wait to find out if a place in the nearby university had been offered, then came the scrimping and saving to afford books and bus fares.

How rewarding it was at the end of three years to receive a graduation certificate. But it didn't stop there, the study bug had got hold and I went on to complete two more degrees. The second degree gave the awesome opportunity to study in Cambridge and excitingly I was there at the same time as my granddaughter who was completing her Master's studies. Occasionally we met up for coffee, we were two very privileged students spanning the generations.

What lights your fire, grips your imagination, makes you think, do you know what, I could do that? Encourage yourself to go beyond your possibilities, you will never know how far you can go until you get there.

As life's natural markers are accomplished and have passed, it may be that suddenly there is a yawning space ahead of you without any defined borders. My mother lived to be 103, my grandmother also lived to a great age, causing me to reflect that should I follow in their pattern. There may be many years ahead that need to be purposeful and have meaning for something bigger than me. There is wisdom in planning as if life stretches forever before you but, living as if today is the moment that counts.

While doing my first degree and getting over anxious about looming exams, my elder daughter reminded me that I had chosen to do this studying, that nobody had pushed me into it, that there were no pressures to find relevant employment at the end of it all. Her final suggestion was that I look at my peer group and consider if they also put themselves under such pressure. So I looked and noted that the most fulfilled of my peer group were those with definite interests, those who had a reason to get out of bed in the morning and have something to look forward to that had meaning.

The next chapter majors on my Camino experience, but sufficient to say here that apart from the amazing sense of achievement at walking about 10 miles a day, steeply uphill for most of the time, and while carrying a heavy backpack, the greatest and most abiding outcome was hearing the stories of so many other pilgrims on the journey. People would walk alongside for a while and tell their stories of pain, blisters and of losing shoes in the horrible sticky black mud. People told deep and meaningful stories of the grief and pain of their lives.

This was not a journey for wimps but for people at a reflective time in life. The awesome privilege was to be trusted with another person's difficult life story. My daughter had a large photo pinned on to the back of her rucksack, a photo of her husband who had died a few months earlier. Observing this gave emotional space for others to talk of difficult loss.

Meanwhile, we had gone beyond anything we thought possible. I am not an athlete or a natural hiker, and others were worried thinking this was a foolish venture 'because of my age'. But we did it. I want to encourage you to discover a new you, one who can go beyond the restraints and ideas that others may have for you. Dare to go beyond it all and then wave your own metaphorical flag in a cheer that declares you did it.

There is a great pleasure in life in doing what people say you cannot do. So what is holding you up?

CHAPTER FIVE

The Camino de Santiago

Third age takes you into new territory.

A long time ago I heard someone say if you want to blossom then get your feet in the flower pot. If you want to go beyond the possibilities then you have to give yourself permission to explore and push beyond your boundaries.

A 97-year-old man recently made the news because he had written a book, an achievement in itself and certainly worth a mention. However, the clue to his real achievement lies between the covers of the book. Around the 60-year-old mark he made a decision to get off the couch and to explore positive physical activities. The couch days firmly behind him, he is now a long-distance walker, has run several marathons and has taken up skiing. He went beyond the possibilities, stopped dreaming, got off the couch and took control of his life.

My own later life 'get off the couch' moment came in 2016 when I took up the challenge to hike 100 kilometres (62 miles) of the famous Spanish Camino de Santiago de Compostela. This ancient pilgrimage route is high in the Galician mountains and has been followed for hundreds of years by countless numbers of 'peregrinos' (pilgrims). Some began their walk way back in the French Pyrenees, while others made a starting point further along the trail in Spain. My own starting point was in Sarria.

Up to this point my later life challenges had been sedentary as I worked my way through three university degrees. Then it became time to take up a new challenge, and on offer was the willingness of my daughter to take up the hike with me; indeed, without her the adventure would not have happened at all.

Of course, you realise, we didn't just put on our boots and start walking, there were many months of preparation, 24 of them actually, but preparation was key to the outcome of the journey. I bought three pairs of hiking boots before being convinced of the suitability of a particular pair. Then for three months I wore the boots all the time, even when in the house, until the boots had moulded to my feet.

I talked with long-distance walkers to learn from their experiences. Probably the most practical and useful advice was to do with Vaseline and two pairs of socks. First smear the feet thickly with Vaseline, wear a pair of hiking sock liners and then a pair of merino hiking socks. The system worked wonderfully; although I fell and damaged both my hip and my ego, there wasn't a scrap of damage to my feet!

Along the way we met too many people debilitated and thwarted by huge blisters. One lady was hospitalised and put on an antibiotic drip. So common was the problem that apparently there was a blister bus, a service provided by volunteers. The bus trawls along the nearest suitable roads offering first aid treatment for damaged feet. There is no doubt that sensible preparation is key to the success or otherwise of the whole venture.

The Camino mirrors life experiences. Just as your third age takes you into a pilgrimage in unfamiliar territory, so the Camino pilgrim, however well prepared and researched, will encounter the unknown. Beyond doubt, my own uncomfortable and rather painful encounter was with a stretch of deep, sticky, black mud. Attempting to navigate myself around the mud while holding on to the branch of a tree, I slipped and fell headlong into the black sticky stuff, face down and with the heavy rucksack on my back preventing me from gaining a grasp of something solid to haul myself up. Unable to reach me to offer help, my daughter was laughing hysterically, though she claims it was just so funny she couldn't help it. To our enormous relief, a very tall agile Australian man came along, and holding on to a sturdy tree he was able to reach out and pull me out of the mud. Convinced that nothing was broken, we continued on our pilgrimage.

You have come to this moment in time and you have to negotiate your own personal journey. Doubtless you will encounter obstacles of the sticky mud kind, and it will be decision time. Will the obstacles defeat you or strengthen your determination to live your dream?

Life has a habit of playing mind games; just as you think it's all sorted in your head, then along comes a guidebook offering an alternative course. A week into our hike, which had been steadily and rather steeply uphill, we checked the guidebook which promised a plateau for the next day. Oh bliss, oh joy, a plateau was just what we needed to give our leg muscles a rest.

Fooled! The next 10 miles were, again, steadily uphill and the disappointment was acute as I mentally composed withering letters to the editor of the book, suggesting he look up the meaning of the word plateau in a dictionary. Your third age pilgrimage will also have such moments. But if your planning was sensible and reasonably well thought out, stick with it, amaze yourself, give a victory punch in the air and shout, 'I did it. Oh my goodness, I did it!'

Much later, and with hindsight, you will realise that your uphill challenge was important; too many plateaus can be boring. While your steep uphill moments will challenge you physically, they will also challenge your thinking and your emotions and, take my word for it, your prayer life will be enhanced.

My Camino plans were to travel as light as possible. Each item going into the backpack was weighed on the kitchen scales and had to be approved as absolutely necessary. There was no need for more than three pairs of socks or undies because each night before putting my aching body on the mattress I washed the socks and undies worn that day and, in the morning, they were pinned on to the backpack to dry in the wind. No need for embarrassment as most other people along the route were doing the same thing.

My daughter and I got a bit snobby about hikers who stayed in hotels and slept in real beds, and no doubt had proper breakfasts. 'Real' pilgrims did it the tough authentic way.

A delightful and remarkably brave German couple, both in their 70s, walked alongside us for a while and shared their story. The husband had bladder and prostate cancer, and under his long trousers was a catheter bag. He was also taking oral chemotherapy drugs. His lovely wife had acute arthritis in both knees which were supported with leather straps bound above and below her knees. On her face she continually wore a serene smile. At the point we met them, this delightful couple had already walked 20 miles a day for four weeks.

This stage of your life is a privilege and won't last forever as the further challenges of ageing will be drawn to your mind. You know the many anxieties that permeate your own situation and lifestyle, but let me convince you that I met so many people in the mountains who knew that illness would shortly curtail their lives. Rather than sitting on the couch dreaming and lamenting for lost opportunities, they strapped on their boots to live out the adventure called life.

Something for you to consider: has your incline become a challenge or an obstacle?

To our surprise, most of the hikers we met were above 50 years old; at age 82 I was regarded as something of a novelty. We discovered that an American man in his early 50s and further along the route told his friends that the walk was too tough and he wanted to quit. Rumours of the 'old lady' who is 82 had reached his friends who told him to walk back and find out if it was true, and if so, then decide whether to quit or to continue. He did find us and, suitably impressed, he continued to walk another 100 kilometres to the final destination at Santiago. We caught up with him there and gleefully shared his excitement and were so proud of him. He did it, and in doing so banked an enormous amount of self-worth and encouragement.

You have already read of the need for preparation for your undertaking, and water was my one thing that I just had to have. Part of each early morning preparations was to make sure my water bottle was filled. Walking in temperatures of 30 degrees plus, I not only drank water but poured it over my head and clothes. As the water seeped in, it provided a blissful if unusual personal air conditioning system.

A valuable, and some might say much-needed, lesson was that of not being so independent. I strive to convince myself that I am capable of meeting my own needs, and I am sure my adult children are grateful while quietly coming alongside in unobtrusive ways. But there were moments in the mountains when I had to concede defeat and even let my daughter carry my rucksack as well as her own. On at least three occasions while going steeply uphill, my daughter almost pulled me up as we each held one end of my walking pole. This is a journey I could never have done on my own. This is a moment for you to think about your own inhibiting factors, to ask yourself what is stopping you from going for gold, and what would make the difference for you to accomplish your goal.

My stubborn independence was challenged in learning to accept the necessity and wisdom of accepting help at strategic moments, such as being pulled up a hill as well as being pulled out of the mud! Consider the lack of preparation that may be holding you back, leaving you to drift through your remaining years with a consequent loss of satisfaction, and work out how to get round that obstacle.

Of course, it isn't always straightforward as you may have family to consider, as well as financial considerations. Not all of my children, or friends, thought that hiking in the mountains was a sensible thing to do at the age of 82. Concerns were expressed such as: 'what if you die?' and 'are you really being responsible?' More positively, my son got himself informed about the Camino, and buying me a Microsoft Band, similar to a Fitbit, he encouraged me to get daily walking fitted in to increase the lengths possible each day. My daughter encouraged me to lengthen my walks and came out walking with me.

It has both fascinated and encouraged me to discover that my adventure had a knock-on effect for other people; it was that response of if I could do it then what could they possibly be encouraged to do?

The Camino also encouraged me to think more widely for myself; if I could hike my Camino then just maybe I can do 'whatever' that something else might be that currently seems so out of reach.

So in this way the pilgrimage continues. This year, 2017, I plan to walk another part of the pilgrimage route; this will be shorter and with marginally less steep uphill inclines. My walking boots are by the front door and my rucksack is on the floor beside me as I type. There might be a problem though, as just three days ago I woke up with no sight in one eye. So until the ophthalmologist works out what the difficulty is the plans may be on hold; meanwhile I plan to continue daily walks wearing my hiking boots, just in case the Camino can really happen.

There have been other positives as a result of my hike. On two occasions I have been invited to speak at meetings and, collaborating with the features editor of our local newspaper, I wrote a centrefold account of my journey and was also asked to write an article for The Open University Alumni magazine.

Not everyone will share your newfound enthusiasms, but do not be deterred, just get yourself properly informed regarding time commitment, any costs, and most arguments will be undermined. Perhaps your chosen venture is to learn to paint – not the kitchen walls, but on the canvas someone gave you last birthday. Full of eagerness you have chosen a spot to set up your easel on a hilltop overlooking stunning views of the Thames estuary. Think it through: first, is it wise to be in an isolated area on your own? And, probably more important, are there any toilets nearby? You get the drift here? Take care of you, it is the small things that can trip you up. Then enjoy!

Just recently a story covered in our local paper told of an 80-year-old lady who was planning to run her fourth marathon. As the story goes, when the lady hit her 60s, she asked herself if that was the time to wind down a gear or to step-up a gear. Stepping-up a gear was the more attractive option so she joined the local running club and, as they say, the rest is history. There is a 'but' here. She made wise preparations; taking wise advice, she ran with a pack of runners. When later wanting to go solo, her daughter joined with her. She made suitable and valid preparation and then set out to live the possibility.

For my Camino there were necessities to buy. First was a suitably lightweight and well-fitted rucksack, then the aforementioned hiking boots and socks. The boots weren't for admiration, not at all, I wore them for three months all the time, both indoors and outside, until they were moulded to my feet. My next important purchase was lightweight waterproof outerwear. In your new venture, whatever form it will take, you just never know when it will rain; not necessarily the wet stuff falling from the sky, but perhaps taking the form of discouragement which could pour all over your head, your studies, your future. You may meet poor advice and envy as well as personal and imposed discouragement, so have a plan to work out in advance what your wet weather gear will look like, what form it will take.

It is what you do with the discouragement that is important, it can even be valuable if you take time to see if there is a kernel of truth that needs addressing. While doing one degree, and not having written an essay for about 50 years, I rather proudly handed in my first assignment to my tutor. Her response came some days later. 'My dear, this is not an essay, it is a suet pudding with too many sultanas unevenly mixed.' Mortified and embarrassed, I slunk away fully aggrieved that the tutor had not noticed the finer points in my work. Did she not realise the hours of research and late night study that had gone into writing the piece she so skilfully rejected? When I crawled out of my bunk hole of humiliation it was to be faced with that moment, yes, that uncomfortable decision-making moment: did I slink away or step-up a gear and continue? Obviously my choice was the upward gear, the one you use when the ride is tough. In all the rest of my studies I never forgot that stinging rebuke. It put some humility into my heart and some backbone into my head and I am forever grateful that the tutor cared enough to make an honest appraisal. She didn't rain on my parade, she opened up the way to make the mists of study dissipate until there was a break in the clouds and it was possible to see the way ahead more clearly. My tutor was one very proud lady when graduation day came.

It is important to emphasise that your chosen project doesn't have to be physical; you don't have to climb up a mountain or go through the rigours of academic study. A dear friend recently retired and, with serious health problems, has reignited her love for art. Her paintings and fine line pencil drawings are a joy and have an honest beauty that matches the intrinsic beauty of the gentle person she is. Gentle, yes, but girthed with backbone and passion.

Wherever possible meet with like-minded people, those who also want to live their lives rather than dream them away in front of a television set. Get to know those who have already walked the path you are choosing and listen to them. Listen as they tell of their mistakes and learn from them; you can't live long enough to make all the mistakes yourself.

CHAPTER SIX

Be an encourager – use your life experiences to encourage others

*The truth is that all through life
we gain new experiences.*

There is a Chinese proverb: If you want one year of prosperity grow grain. If you want 10 years of prosperity grow trees. If you want 100 years of prosperity then grow people.

In the classroom of life you have learned more than a few things – so what do you do with them? You could pack them in a trunk in the attic, you could display them on a shelf in the sitting room, or you can use them as an aid to be a constructive, compassionate encourager walking alongside someone else on their life journey. This can be a life-enhancing experience for you as you walk alongside, remembering not to lead, or to push, but reaching out alongside with steadiness and empathy.

Here is a thought for you as you consider the above suggestion: getting older isn't an opt-out opportunity from life, it is an opt-in opportunity to build on everything you have become in the many tangles of positivity, negativity, and also the input from wiser people than you.

Maya Angelou, author, Black American activist, wise woman and all-round encourager, offered this advice: just do the right thing, live what you teach, be the best person you can be, don't live with regrets, get out there and make a difference. You know that words have power, so handle them with care.

Somehow, sometimes it seems that getting to where you are now crept up on you while you weren't looking. Without your permission, it seems that while you were asleep someone stole the real you full of youth and energy and left behind a person you don't recognise when you look in the mirror. Now is the time to take control of what happens to the rest of your life, especially these special years before you get to that other part – also called the rest of your life. In the final chapter of this book you will find some helpful guides to books or websites that can motivate you should you be short on ideas.

Meanwhile, push yourself beyond the parameters of the past, both good and bad; use the knowledge gained as building steps to enable not only your dreams but also the hopes of others. While this is your time to explore, to allow yourself to make mistakes, to take risks and to learn from them, it is also a time for getting alongside that other person, that someone else who needs encouragement and, in so doing, you are refusing to sell yourself short.

A word of warning: being an encourager for others is not the opportunity to turn into a grumpus. For sure, there are tremendous differences in the way you have lived your younger life and the way life is lived for young people today. But! There is no need to dwell on it. Leave grumpy to the old grumps who get paid to be so on television; this is not your calling in life, it isn't your aim. If you accept the challenge to be an encourager, then you have two aims: one is to encourage yourself to be a bigger, better, more compassionate and encouraging version of yourself; then to be that amazing person who is a delight to be around and who can think healthily of using life's learned skills to bless someone else's life.

Yes, you have got a little older, but can you remember what it was like to be a child, to be a teenager, to be a young parent? The world has changed beyond anything that resembles your younger years, but some things never change and one of them is the need to be understood, to be listened to non-judgmentally. These are experiences common to humanity in general.

A need to talk and to be listened to is evidenced by the modern phenomenon of indiscreet use of the mobile phone. 'Please listen to me,' seems to shriek out from unguarded lips on the bus, the pavement, the train and even in the bank. My own experience of riding on the bus is that mobile users not only need to be heard but also to attract as wide as possible an audience of unwilling bus passengers.

It is common to mankind to have our words out there hanging in the air for someone to latch on to and to listen, but further in this chapter we will look at more appropriate ways of doing that.

At this moment just start with yourself and what you have to offer in terms of learned skills. First, you are alive and breathing – that is a good start. You are breathing the fine air of planet Earth that in itself is a gift and an advantage point from which to engage in your mission – that is if you should choose to accept the challenge to be an encourager.

Be prepared, get your toolkit out, because there will be times when you feel knocked back or discouraged – that will be the time to open up that box of experiences and recognise that despite the knocks you are here now with the opportunity to use those tools to help build, bit by bit, part of someone else's life.

Life itself is a tool which has provided you with skills. Exploring the jungles of the world might not be for you; however, just a peep into the life tools you have will mark out for you one marked 'talk'. That word earned its place in the box from the times you remember when you longed for someone to talk to, for someone who would non-judgmentally listen to you, for someone to give you the gift of just being available. That tool in your box is highly polished because you will remember there were many tough times when, although you didn't realise it, you were being honed with a gift to use for others. Your learned gifts may be very practical – as a wood-turner for example, a gardener or handyman. Perhaps you spent years in accountancy or training to be a teacher. You have hidden reserves to draw on, depths of experiences that have prepared you to be an encourager. In the next chapter we can talk about the skills required to enable you to be a listener; I can tell you, there is a world shortage of listeners.

The bigger picture here is that because of your adult formative years you have a lot to offer, and in doing so, you are also passing on something of yourself that will have its part in the future.

You have learned so much on your journey from teenage years, possible fractured relationships, the longing for someone to just understand you – not to solve your problems but to just listen and be an empathising presence, a metaphorical arm around your shoulder. I guess reading these words will evoke strong memories; perhaps you are remembering how, as part of the post-war generation, you had to make do and mend. Scrimping and saving were part of the common, and shared, culture. Are you remembering when it was so easy to get a job, and if you didn't like it, to walk out and almost immediately get another job? It's not like that anymore.

Yet, still, whatever the age or culture, human beings have similar basic needs, such as the anxiety of 'Will I fit in? Will I fall in love? Does anybody out there care?' I am sure you can tap into many of those things. Yes, even if you find it difficult to understand the apparent casualness of the culture of today, don't be fooled; the young, and even the older, are adept at clothing their true selves behind masks while they retain the basic human longing to be affirmed.

Perhaps again, it is wise to start with yourself, encourage yourself to recognise that you are a survivor in this strange thing we call life. And use your survival skills to be an enabler, an encourager, a means of security to that other person who comes your way. Remind yourself that you have a lifetime of experience and skills to use to make a valuable contribution. On the other hand, it might just be the kindness of your words that will make a difference as you say, 'Well done you.'

It may be that you are reading this on a day when everything is just too much bother, when you want to shout at the printed page and say, 'You don't understand how defeated I feel, how tired I am, how many family and work pressures there are on my life.' You are right, I don't know, but this I know from experience, that sometimes all that is required is to move one foot, to put that one foot in front of the other and gently move. You may not be able to do this physically but you can do it in your heart, to be that person who makes an effort. Also there are times when the sensible thing to do is to have some sleep! Very often the most honest and encouraging gift of encouragement is simply a smile. A smile freely given will warm your own heart and put a bit of bounce back into your own step.

Elsewhere in this book I have mentioned the severely handicapped lady who functions as a counsellor, as a listener and encourager. She has gone beyond her own difficulties to provide that added extra which can make a difference in someone else's time of need; it is about empathising with the deep-felt need that many people have to just be encouraged. You will have experienced how helpful it can be to unclutter your thinking and your emotions when you have the opportunity to verbalise the worrisome and troubling things that impinge on life sometimes. Listening to your own words hanging in the air helps to make sense of your thoughts; it helps you to discard any nonsense and to enhance the possible.

Encouraging and listening are attributes with much in common. A few years ago I ditched the car and became a regular commuter on the local buses. You want an education in the art of being an encourager or of listening? Can't afford to go on a course? Get on a bus! You want to learn how to be an encourager or listener in a non-judgmental manner? Get on a bus, all of life teems on there.

My bus journey takes me through an area of deprivation and a high proportion of people with learning difficulties. Over the years some good friendships have been formed. The bus also picks up passengers from some of the many local sheltered complexes housing old people whose lifetime peer group has died off and who long for someone to just listen, and on the bus they have a captive audience in whoever comes to sit nearby.

So, all you need to do is get on the bus, pay your fare, sit down and listen; in doing so you will probably make someone's day and you will have learned a lot about what makes life tick for marginalised people. You may have lightened the sorrow of someone who is weary with grief. You may have the opportunity to affirm a young mum who is struggling to contain a baby, two toddlers, the pushchair and all her shopping. Also, in that moment when you offer up your seat to someone whose need is greater than yours, you may bring a moment of affirmation, of acceptance and relief to the humdrum of another passenger. But that is not the end of your bus travel experiences. There is history in old people – they tell stories of lives that are unlikely to ever be replicated, lives more burdensome but also slower in pace. Listen and learn.

My bus stop friends include a 60-year-old woman who has the mental age of a six-year-old. She is out and about most days as her support worker takes her shopping or to an exercise class. Invariably when I meet them this child-lady will proudly show me her new shoes, her new bag or the grazes on her knees from her latest fall. Her day has been gladdened, her support worker enjoys the momentary respite, and my day has been enriched as the encounter makes me realise how very blessed my life is.

Another bus stop friend is about 80, let's call her Ivy, her husband has Parkinson's disease and dementia and all too often Ivy is overwhelmed with fatigue and distress. Bit by bit she has told me her life story while waiting at the bus stop and on the journey into town. One day, as I neared the bus stop, she called out for help, for me to hold her hand because she was having a panic attack. It was as we sat together and I encouraged slow deep breathing till she recovered that the beginning of a friendship was formed.

Lately Ivy's son has walked with her to the bus stop and while waiting he has filled in many other parts of the life they have shared as a family. As he talks there emerges a story of teenage romance, of wartime deprivation and the bombing of their home; of their move to the new town and a life starting all over again as they moved away from everything that was familiar. The son affectionately refers to his mother as 'a poor little cow who used to carry the scrag ends of meat wrapped in newspaper all tucked under her arm'. There you go, a history lesson from the recent past at the bus stop.

So you still want to learn the skills of listening and encouragement but can't afford the course fees? Learn on the job, get on a bus and your fellow travellers will teach you and all with a history lesson thrown in.

Use the opportunities that life puts in your path. For example, if you should live in an area that in times past might have been called a sink estate and you overhear a young mum talking quietly and encouragingly to her child rather than the all too often heard abusive language of 'git yerself 'ere you rotten git'. Hey, what a moment to be an encourager as, with a few kind words while admiring the child, your very presence of affirmation can be the kindest gift the young mum will have that day. Then move on and be watchful for the next opportunity. Remember that a smile costs nothing and when you smile, even if you don't feel like it, you feel better while becoming the brightness in a space of bleakness.

The memory of a smile can last for ever – well perhaps all day, yet it can't be bought or sold and only has value when given away. So if you didn't start the day with a smile it's not too late to start practising ready for tomorrow. That bit of wisdom came off a bookmark received one year.

Let me tell you about another bus journey, and this one was not so clever. My seat was in front of a young lady who was talking on her mobile phone; she was telling her friend that she had the results from her Master's degree and that she had passed. Then, in the kind of loud voice reserved for use when on the mobile phone, she told the tale of both her mother and sister who were having affairs, even naming the men involved. Believe me, you could almost hear the hairs on the necks of all the other passengers pop right up. The young lady and I alighted at the same stop and I approached her with congratulations for passing her Master's degree. Then, as she enjoyed the compliment, I continued with 'but' and outlined how mortified her mother and sister would be if they knew that she had told a busload of people about their affairs. I had been a reluctant listener to her story so decided it gave me permission to be part of the conversation and, of course, you may think that I might not have been right. On the whole, I think you can only get away with that kind of conversation if you look ancient and speak with gentle kindness.

Was I wise? Maybe not, but the young lady hopefully learned a lesson that day from someone who had lived a lot longer and could see the potential damage. Isn't it odd that when using their phones in a public space all too often the users are unaware that others around them are listening – and would rather not? That is not the kind of useful listening the next chapter aims to address.

If you are having a bad day, give yourself a talking to – be your own encourager and do something positive. Elsewhere I have told of the day when feeling very miserable I went out deliberately looking for at least three opportunities to make another person feel better about themselves. It wasn't too difficult. The lady on customer care in the supermarket had an ear to ear grin when I commented on her unusual nail varnish.

When all else fails, smile. Have you noticed how many people walk along looking at the pavement? A quick 'Hello' and a smile might be a shock to them but just might make them smile too and walk a bit taller.

A strategy I have used on a downcast day is to buy a bunch of flowers then wander around working out who to give them to. Just imagine the amazement you would feel if someone approached you with such an unexpected gift. One morning on the way to college and feeling deflated about exam results, I gave a bunch of flowers to the bus driver. His astonishment was brilliant as he held up the flowers to show them to the busload of passengers before passing the gift on to an elderly lady who, in her turn, smiled with delight and said she was going to tell her husband the flowers were from her toy boy.

There are opportunities to perform random acts of kindness. Make someone's day, brighten the moment with a smile or positive word; these are gifts you can freely give away when your purse is empty. However, your enthusiastic moment could be misinterpreted so don't be disheartened. I can well imagine that to be greeted with an unexpected gift or greeting can be a bit startling.

CHAPTER SEVEN

Loneliness eased with the gift of listening

To listen, to be allowed in the inner places of another's life is a privilege.

Can you recall moments when you longed for someone, anyone, to just listen to you? That someone didn't need to have the answers to your situation, but, for you, just being able to talk, to be listened to in a non-judgmental manner, was a gift at a needful moment in life. Listening is an asset, and is a great gift for you to utilise at whatever stage of life you are at. To listen, to be allowed in the inner places of another's life, is a privilege.

A brief interlude here – here is a thought and a useful tip for you when needing to summarise your writing. Perhaps you are writing your Sunday sermon, or writing an essay for your college tutor, or even writing an important email that has rather too much detail or information and you just can't work out how to summarise so that you don't let the reader get lost in a fog of words. Get on a bus is my advice! Listening to my fellow passengers I soon discovered how much of their life story could be covered in 15 minutes.

I also discovered that many older people, and by that I mean people from 50 years upwards, travel on the bus just to have some company. I also discovered that retirees, lost for the companionship of the workplace, would take themselves into the town centre where, equipped with a packed lunch and a book, they would sit on a bench waiting for someone to come along and be a willing participant in a conversation.

In this way I heard a lot of interesting detail about the evolving manner in which our town was built. There were people who moved from the east end of London, who although not many miles away were homesick for the familiar friendships and places. Other people had taken the opportunity to move to a new town to a new house on a new estate. Yet once the advantages had been explored, a longing for the familiar emerged, a longing for the neighbourhood friendships. And so it was that lonely people found a way to have a conversation with anyone who would listen to the stories of loss and felt isolation. To be a listener in such a situation was to offer a gift, and in the giving also to be enriched by the history embedded in the lives of others.

Being a careful listener might come naturally to you, but if not, it is a skill you can develop. In the final chapter of this book you will find details of courses available for those keen to learn.

It isn't all about old people; let me tell you a story, a true one. One day, while I was sitting on the bus for a rather long journey, a young man alighted and sat in the only vacant seat, which happened to be next to an old lady. By old, I mean she was easily about 80 years old. The young man smelt. His appearance was of the kind you would not want to meet on a lonely lane on a dark night, and as he swaggered up the aisle, he stuck two fingers up at another passenger. There didn't seem to be an obvious reason why, only he knew the reason for that.

But something magical happened as he sat next to the rather prim and neat old lady. Her whole demeanour was calm as, with hands quietly placed on her lap, she smiled at the young man. Within minutes he had calmed down as he began to tell his story to the quiet listener beside him. The young man seemed to have a fractured relationship with his family, his erstwhile girlfriend had recently had a baby, his, but wouldn't allow him access. As he unfolded his story he became calmer, until about half an hour later as his quiet listener got up to leave the bus, there was evidence of a still rapport between them. I often wonder about those two people who were so casually caught up in each other's lives, and I wonder what impact the gift of being listened to had on the young man who had loneliness wrapped around him like unforgiving cling film.

To be allowed into the inner sanctum of another person's life is an honour. Of course, you may be reading this and thinking that this is not your calling in life because you can't keep a secret. No problem, you will have your own special gifts to offer as an encourager; perhaps you can plant daffodils or forget-me-nots on the spare patch of ground nearby. If history is your passion, or if you are doing a late life degree in psychology, or even if you have nothing else planned for this phase of your life, get on a bus.

Of course, you already know that listening isn't about giving advice but rather allows space for the other person to hear themselves speak and, in doing so, to formulate their own thought patterns, options and ideas, and maybe even come up with their own solutions.

Recently I listened to a lady who had been in three disastrous relationships. Giving her the space to get her own words out of the futility of her mind and into a sheltered secure space, she heard herself and began to diagnose her own dilemma, thus allowing herself to see a way forward.

Did you know that all this listening stuff can have two-way connotations? Taking on the role of an active listener validates the worth of your own life lessons; it affirms the self while giving meaning to all the hiccups of your life, no matter how large or small. Your life is being given added value. While being exposed to the life thoughts of the other, it is even possible for you, the listener, to be challenged about dearly held assumptions; remember it is never too late to learn, to become the person you could have been or long to be.

This gift you are using may nudge you to reflect on your own life, including the opportunities lost and the opportunities gained. It isn't all about someone else; it can offer you time for wise reflection as you acknowledge past benefits, advantages and are grateful.

Not all of those reflections will gladden your heart, but the reality check may be a prompt towards dealing with regrets in a meaningful way. You will have discovered that when you are being quietly still and listening it is not only your ears, but also your heart, your brain, your empathy, your body language and your focus that are being called on to work together. Happy listening!

CHAPTER EIGHT

Bridging the generations (young people)

A word aptly spoken is like apples of gold in settings of silver.

~ King Solomon

A social media young people's site discussed the difference between the young and old generations; it read that both generations are needed for what they are able to contribute to society. The younger people question, challenge and spark change. The older people put on the brake sometimes, providing the wisdom of experience that can help with wise decision-making.

Just for a moment we are back to the listening, encouraging roles. And some of this you have already read but it is worth repeating. Can you remember how when you were truly young, maybe a teenager or a young parent, sometimes there was a deep longing for someone to just let you talk without being judged? And you may remember how desperately awful it felt to be misunderstood or unfairly judged when you had made honest mistakes, or even those deliberate mistakes you had made without realising what the consequences could be?

Maybe you remember how, as a teenager, you just knew that you knew everything and wondered why adults, in particular your parents, were so dumb? These are helpful memories to hold on to when you are bewildered by today's very different life culture offered to young people. You know that feeling when you are bewildered by the use of earphones, by the use of hands-free phones, and you wonder if the culprits are suffering some sort of madness as they apparently talk into thin air? After all, in your day, back then, if someone walked about talking to themselves the men in white coats from the local hospital might have been called.

On my first day in Cambridge as I tried to find the college, I asked a young woman for directions. She almost snarled her reply, 'Can't you see I'm on the phone?' Well, actually, no. There wasn't a phone to be seen. That was my first introduction to the weird and wonderful world where people appear to be having one-sided conversations.

I am sure you recollect that when you were a teenager or novice young adult, respect and criticism didn't go well together and may have compounded the difficulty already being faced. It is helpful to remember those awkward encounters – painful maybe, but useful.

A word of caution, and I may be teaching my grandmother to suck eggs, but remember to avoid judgmental responses, and also to avoid switching off while mentally writing your shopping list; and if you really must say something, gentle kindness are the words which come to mind at this moment. Reputably the wisest man who ever lived, King Solomon, said that a word aptly spoken is like apples of gold in settings of silver.

A big question confronting you at this stage in life, with retirement either in place or looming, could be simply, 'What now?' You have learned so much and in that learning you have a legacy to leave for those coming up behind you. Of course, this is also your time to enjoy yourself, a time for all those hobbies or pursuits there was never time for before. Even so, you may be feeling the need to do something more than days of relaxation and personal enjoyment. It has to be recognised that not every person can begin to contemplate such leisure as many are caught up in caring capacities, perhaps looking after grandchildren or elderly parents.

Nonetheless, the likelihood of being called upon to be those wise listening ears to a younger generation is almost certain unless you live in isolation far away from civilisation. Even on my Camino challenge and walking for a while with pilgrims of other nationalities (indeed we only met two English people), my ears, my heart and my past life experiences were called on, and while most people we met were midlife upwards, we did meet a delightful young Italian man. His story was heart-warming.

With all the above in mind, it is worth taking a look again at some of the necessities packed into that toolkit called life. I think that respect comes first, second and last. To respect anyone of any age is a starting point to encouragement. However, you have to get your head around the fact that today's young people live in a vastly changing world. Perhaps your world was scary for other reasons, but whatever those reasons were it is useful knowledge which provides you with another tool as a non-judgmental, non-critical listener and encourager.

No matter how different from today your scary moments were, they fuelled the urgency and sickening fear of an adrenaline rush, the cold clammy uncertainty that took the strength from your legs. Constant news items blaring out about the possibility of a nuclear war or a cold war with Russia may have caused you great anxiety and uncertainty not so very different from those of today.

Although the anxieties of today may have different labels, among them are the current revelations of high-profile abuse and lies, the constant barrage of awfulness that emanates from the Middle East; such things leave not only us but our young people with questions about who we can trust. All of these events produce the same metaphorical rush of adrenaline and sickening anxiety. You have experienced this before and now is the opportunity to retain a wise head and the listening ears that can be a very necessary and cooling balm for others. You have been there and have survived.

Every generation has faced its painful threats, yet each generation has produced people who didn't dissolve, neither did they just dream, but with a lot of self-encouragement and encouragement from others who had walked that path before, they clung on to and even dared to live their dreams.

It is possible that some of the criticism directed towards young people derives from a twinge of envy. There wasn't a phone in your house, in your road or maybe not even in your town. And when your home did acquire such a luxury the phone was on a party line and shared with perhaps two or three other houses. My teenage granddaughter listened in disbelief when I explained the gymnastics involved in making a phone call 'when I was her age' but I also reminded her that one day she would be my current age, and possibly she would be talking with her own granddaughter who, in turn, would also listen in astonishment as she was informed that 'when I was your age we had to carry our phones around in our pockets.' Gadgetry and electronics will have advanced to a degree that we can only dare to imagine. Or perhaps would prefer not to imagine.

It is worth taking a moment to think again about criticism, and memories. Remember how difficult it was to be criticised. Social media has taken criticism to a different level and our young people, as well as their elders, too easily become the target of disdain – for example, criticism of the clothes they wear, or almost don't wear. Perhaps your moment of teenage fashion rebellion was to join in with those who chose to wear their cardigans back to front. And you tried to pretend you were not mortified if someone stared then drew your attention to it.

You may feel that social media has a lot to answer for, and I would agree. When people called you names you probably leered back at them chanting 'sticks and stones may break my bones but names will never hurt me.' Of course name calling did hurt you and you may have wept for a week but then you got on with what you were supposed to be doing: learning and living. But now the remorseless, cruel tormenting of social media, insidiously thrown from so many strands, makes a lie of the notion that 'names can never hurt me' and on a daily level there is news of young, truly young, people hanging themselves. The repellent damage being done has coined a phrase 'The Snowflake Generation'. This book doesn't pretend to have any answers or advice but just draws attention to the immense sadness of it all.

As a third ager you may not have teenagers on the horizon of your thinking or ambitions right now, but you can be sure that, sought after or not, those encounters will arise from someone somewhere so it is worthwhile being prepared.

Just like you, my growing-up years were in a now forever lost age, yet it was not all that long ago really in the scheme of things, but in terms of change, it seems to be many light years ago.

My childhood years were during World War II which blighted so many lives, yet also forged backbone and determination. New clothes were a rarity, a weekly bath was a shared occasion with other siblings. The word fashion wasn't yet part of our vocabulary. The ME generation had not arrived, teenagers were only defined in the era of the Beatles, but we were a generation whose life experiences toughened us up.

Walking to work, or to wherever else, was our exercise and didn't require gym payments. Political correctness had not yet hit our locality. The nanny state was unheard of and children could play in the streets. Yes, things have changed, and seemingly, too fast, and never before in our western culture have we experienced such an onslaught, emotionally and mentally, that is damaging our younger people.

Your toolkit of life skills can truly make the difference between a positive life experience for others, or not. You get to choose. This book is not a psychological tool to equip the eager learner, rather this book is written from one life learner to another and to encourage you to see the attributes you have which can be used, if you so wish, to enable someone else. Your someone else may be one person or a whole heap of people.

Your world now is one in a hurry; the pace of life has become fast and urgent. Sometimes it all seems so fast that, as already noted, it is as if tomorrow comes before yesterday. However, one thing that has not changed is the need to be understood and acknowledged as a valid person of worth on planet Earth. A swift nod and 'How are you?' doesn't quite meet the need.

The world you knew has changed in so many ways, there is even a new word to describe the generation currently in the age 18 to 24 bracket, it is called The Millennials, a group often perceived negatively by others. These are people mainly highly skilled and versed in the electronic era. Usually their lives are bounded by social media. They are the first generation born into a life of the internet and consequent technologies. Yet, at the core there remains the human need to be understood and valued.

Dear third ager, if you are at a loss to know just where your life goes from this moment on, when retirement possibly leaves a yawning void begging the question of what do you do next, one option is to use your life experiences to build into the life of someone coming up behind you. There is a personal advantage to this.

As your wise and patient listening allows another person to develop and grow, something of yourself is being taken into the future as you become part of the building block of another generation.

CHAPTER NINE

Only you

*We are fools to try to hold on to what can only
be enhanced by giving away or sharing.*

You have come to this time in life with many possibilities and a wealth of expertise, and you know that to get older is a privilege. As the unique, one-off human being that you are, think how this knowledge of all that you are will affect not only your today but also your remaining years. In many ways, it is a personal choice to decide if, or how, you will take hold of the moment, of the decisions concerning your own future. Obviously, other people and life circumstances will make their mark and you will have to factor in all those other elements, keeping them in tension as you go forward. To have arrived at the third age stage of life you have already experienced so much; how you use those experiences for good or ill will mostly be your choice.

At this stage you will have realised that your own life challenges are set to force you into a new stage of maturity and growth. Even though you may anticipate many years ahead of you, there is still something worthwhile about making the most of the present moment without being entangled by regrets of the past, or of concerns about the future. While you need to make lifelong plans you can also learn to live each day, with all its downsides or opportunities, as if it is your last day on planet Earth. One day it really will be your last day so make the most of every breathable opportunity. Give away your smiles and encouragement as if you have a truckload of the stuff that keeps getting refilled with each breathtaking delight you give away. Be generous with your heart attitudes.

Your life is a gift, so live each moment, don't just dream it. All the thoughts of 'if only' you had more money, better health, more encouragement, a bigger house, won't change your circumstances, but you alone have the choice to decide how to give meaning to the life you have. It is still true that a smile costs nothing except some minor adjustment of the muscles in your face. It remains true that only you can choose to be an encourager or a doom-monger.

If you have a personal faith you already know that the love of God is not meant as an asset just to benefit yourself but is a vehicle to reach out with blessing into the lives of others. The acceptance, kindness and relationship of your spiritual life finds its fulfilment in recognising that these are gifts from God to reach out to others through you. A great and awesome privilege!

We have already noted the possibility that right now you are seething through gritted teeth muttering, 'But you don't know the circumstances of my life.' True, I don't, but this I do know, that we are fools to try to hold on to what can only be enhanced by giving away or sharing.

Perhaps you don't feel unique, but you are. No one else can ever be the unique combination of genetic input that makes you who you are. No one else has lived your life experiences that make you the right person at the right time to be alongside someone else. No one else but you at this moment in time can be the person who sometime today will meet someone else and either bless their day with a word of encouragement or a smile or... ? Only you.

I read this account of an amazing attitude that had been observed by a young woman. She starts by saying:

> *Be kind to yourself...* then continues:
> *I grew up on a small family farm, with plants and animals needing care in every direction, so holidays were rare. But one summer my parents convinced a neighbouring farmer to tend to our goats and chickens while we got to go to the beach for a whole entire week. On the morning we departed my mother stripped her bed, washed and dried the*

linen and remade the bed perfectly, just as if she were preparing it for a guest. I was baffled. Nobody was going to be visiting while we were away; why go to so much time and trouble?

'Oh,' my mother explained, when I asked her why she had bothered, 'this is just a little present I am giving my future self. This way, when she comes home all tired and worn out at the end of her holiday, she'll have the gift of fresh clean sheets waiting to welcome her back to her own bed.'

'She' my mother had said – not 'I'. I found it striking that she felt such friendly kindness towards the person she would be. My mother's current self clearly believed that the stranger she'd become over the next week was deserving of love. This gift of a freshly made bed was not an insignificant act. It was a conscious handshake of affection across time, a way of connecting the woman of this moment to the woman of the future.

There is a lesson here well worth remembering: a well-known and often quoted scripture is to love others as we love ourselves. It is so easy to remember the bit about 'loving others' but somehow you don't readily notice the words 'as you love yourself'.

Here is a question important to consider: where/who/what do you want to be in 10 years' time? An obvious answer is that you want to be alive. So put the mileage in now. Eat properly, be active, use your brain, be an active participant in life; your family, your friends, being a volunteer, just do something that has you interacting socially. Of course, you can always get on a bus!

The organisation Age UK has highlighted that loneliness increases the risk of dementia, depression and Type 2 diabetes. There can be no substitute for positive social interaction. So why not go out on a limb where the fruit is? Find out what clubs, societies and groups exist in your locality. The University of the Third Age is a gift just waiting to be explored. Your local library should have the details you need.

A North Carolina State University study showed that over 60s who were happy, optimistic and, importantly, felt useful, were better equipped to deal with stress.

The difficulties and disappointments of life can be re-worded as challenges and opportunities. Even the frail and housebound can be encouragers, or not! My elderly mother lived in Australia, and eventually, when she was in deteriorating health, my brother suggested it was time I made the long journey to visit her. After 24 hours' flying time, my first ever flying experience, I arrived at mother's bungalow to be met with grumpiness, criticism and put-downs. Four weeks later I flew home, but this only after jumping to her every critical word, clearing out cupboards, weeding her large garden etc., and all the time hearing her constant mantra, 'No one ever comes near or by, no one does anything to help when you are old.' She had two sons nearby who actually did call near or by!

Arriving back home, admittedly rather fed up and tired, I went to visit an elderly aunt thinking that she would like to have news of Mother and her life in Australia. Aunty also had a mantra, 'No one ever comes near or by when you are old...' For the next few days I wandered around thinking that surely my name was Nobody. Get a grip now while you still can and practise pleasantry with all the delightful offshoots it can produce.

How very different those scenarios could have been, I am sure you can paint another more wholesome picture. Are you thinking at this point that I have forgotten this book is meant to be about SuperAgers? No! But you, we, all of us are in training for that next stage of life which will come as surely as night follows day; hopefully practice now will make perfect then.

There is often news about the loneliness of elderly people including the reality that many will have gone for perhaps two weeks without speaking to anyone. A telephone befriending service in the UK has been set up to ensure that a frail elderly person receives at least one phone call a week, just to chat. Please don't shoot me when you read this next bit, but I do just wonder that if someone has the strength to pick up the phone for an incoming call and talk for a few minutes, that just maybe they could be the person who would pick up the phone to make an outgoing call. To be the one who makes some other person's day. Perhaps that is too simplistic.

Thinking of phone calls, you know how some of life's lessons have been gained from listening to the (? legitimate) complaints of others of your peer group; comments such as: 'His mother never makes the first contact, she expects us to phone her every week but she never bothers to pick up the phone and ask how we are, how the grandchildren are...' Get the picture? Your third age years are the time to build some new good habits in preparation for those later years. Of course, there are many elderly parents who don't make those phone calls because they know that their sons or daughters work very long hours and already have little special time at home with their family, but read on.

Postage stamps are getting rather pricey, but buying one a week, or one a month, could be reasonable, then write a letter or card just to say 'Thinking of you'... in whatever the circumstance might be. Of course, by the time you get old, email, Facebook and Twitter, those alternative means of communication, will have disappeared to be replaced by some other means as yet not thought of. Oh dear, I digress.

A workout exercise of life was when you learned more about yourself, of those moments that took you by surprise, perhaps things you were unaware of. My mother was Italian, a race of very voluble people who have the habit of all talking at the same time. In our house to make yourself heard was simple, you just talked rather louder and with a lot of hand gesticulations. And all these years later I still do it, and am unable to break the deeply ingrained habit. My daughters think I am butting in, and of course I am, but in the context of my upbringing it wasn't butting in, it was being part of the conversation. So I have learned, or rather am still learning, that when with a group of people it is best for me not to talk at all, then I can't get it wrong. Going off to do the washing-up is a useful ploy. What is your problem? Don't all shout at once, just drop me an email.

Let's be positive, now may be the time to discover that stubborn streak of hope that if you just turn up in life with a good heart, light will dawn in unexpected ways. Just don't give up. Persevere and you will surprise and encourage yourself. Often courage in the difficult times is just about that proverbial putting one foot in front of the other as you learn more about the things you can keep and the things it might be time to change.

Don't underestimate yourself, you are built for growth not for stagnation. You are built to discover ways to fulfil that deep-felt need to give back to society, and in doing so to build your own markers. Remember that every day above ground is a good one and every new morning is a gift, every breath is a fresh opportunity.

There isn't a cure for getting older, but to explore this midlife time can be an adventure, which the dictionary defines as *'being uncertain of the outcome'*, and it also alters the mindset from the negative 'Oh dear' to 'Yes, let's get going'.

If already you are thinking big and bold, even if tentatively, then you are alive and on the journey of life. If health problems get in the way, find an alternative route and remember this: never, never apologise for health problems, just accept that they are there and that there is no need to draw attention to it – it just means that your life has taken on different parameters which need exploring. Another apology you can live without: when health or age make you feel a nuisance, don't apologise, sometimes it's all right to accept that maybe you are a nuisance, but not one of your making. A warm 'Thank you' for the help offered in those situations has much happier overtones.

Have you spent your years full of envy for the stick-thin models like Twiggy or envied the youthful seductiveness of the curvy Betty Grable? It's time to get over it because the body which has carried the real you and all your dreams is the only one you have, so be kind to it, nurture it and don't say unkind things to it. Don't call it names like dumpy, fat, thin, gawkish; no, no, rather be kind to it because it is going to see you on many adventures yet. In the final chapter you will find further information and advice including a snazzy new book by the Green Goddess, Diana Moran, *Sod Sitting, Get Moving*.

And a bit of extra encouragement: looked at honestly, you will know in your heart that you are not entirely self-made; your companions along the way, be they family, friends, work colleagues or neighbours, have all intervened. So now as you handle yourself with care you are also in the process of helping to inform the life of someone else.

You have learned not to sweat the small stuff. You have learned what things are really important and that not everything needs to be turned into World War III. Years ago when my children were small, and before I had learned about not sweating the small stuff, my nine-year-old son was refusing to eat the cauliflower on his plate at lunch time – the meal we used to call dinner before it got stolen and placed later in the day. Back to the story – I foolishly said, 'Well, no one is leaving the table till your dinner is finished.' 'No one' meant either young son or me. Four hours later we were still sitting there and I had to concede defeat. Hopefully you have done better and chosen your skirmishes more wisely.

Research has shown that tiny achievable shifts in your habits make a big difference and those tiny bits are a good place to start. Successful dieters know this truth well; those who lose weight right and maintain the loss are those who began by making small mindset and habit changes.

Here is a helpful mantra for you, 'I believed I could so I did'; it is much better than 'I could never do that.' When I fell in the mud on my Camino journey and wondered what I thought I was doing on this trail, I remembered my daughter-in-law. At about the age of 40, she said, 'I have never ridden a bike.' That may sound harmless you think, but oh no, her husband, my son, always an over the top enthusiast, decided that of course she could learn to ride a bike, and not only could she learn to ride a bike but she could ride one all the way from Land's End on the far corner edge of southern England to John o' Groats in the far north of Scotland. But it doesn't stop there; they had four young children, their ages ranging from seven to 14, and they also were put on a training programme to do the aforementioned ride. Crazy? Absolutely yes, but even that is not all; early in the ride my daughter-in-law fell off her bike, had to go to hospital to have injuries to her arm sorted out, then, would you believe? She got back on the bike and completed the task. She believed she could, so she did. She was my hero when I fell in the mud and wondered what to do.

Because you are looking after the person you will be in 10 years' time, it can be sensible to do a bit of research and find out what the best resources are available to meet your needs. Let's assume that overhauling your diet is a start, next you decide to start walking to strengthen your bones and also to work towards warding off Type 2 diabetes and oiling your creaky joints while enhancing your energy levels and dealing with stress. All those benefits, and you only started off with one simple habit change.

If you need some more encouragement, did you know that strengthening your muscles can help to increase the levels of protein needed to generate new brain cells while also improving muscles of your older brain cells? Again, do your own research, but meanwhile pick up the weights or a can of beans, do some lifting and start to make a difference.

If you still need convincing, you will discover that while exercise helps to ward off Type 2 diabetes, it is also mood-enhancing. It has been shown that a 10-minute walk after each meal is beneficial, especially after a carb-heavy meal. Walking doesn't have to be a nip round the block in pouring rain, it can include going up and down the stairs a few times.

Midlifers need to be aware that alcohol damages the liver more easily the older you get, so do yourself a favour and cut back, save some money and do yourself good.

What can I say? All these benefits have accrued just because you chose to make one small change. Congratulations!

However, there is yet more; consider that often it is necessary to lay aside the regrets and mistakes of the past. For sure, learn from them, put right where you can, then walk away leaving yourself free to explore this new territory and live your dreams.

Did you know that diabetes increases the risk of gum disease? It has also been demonstrated that gum disease can raise blood glucose levels and then it's full circle back to the diabetes. So go to the dentist regularly, clean your teeth at least the minimal numbers of times a day – that being twice. Buy new toothbrushes and be the person it is nice to sit next to on the bus... no halitosis.

But that is not the end of the tooth tale. It is now known that plaque on the teeth not only damages the teeth but can contribute towards an unwanted heart attack by increasing inflammation of your artery linings. Poor dental health is implicated in cognitive decline and is also responsible for causing mental efficiency to deteriorate more rapidly. Want to live your dream? Buy that new toothbrush and go to the dentist regularly.

And to end this chapter let us have a look at fashion – not the clothes you wear but the other stuff you clothe yourself with. What not to wear includes the weight of the world on your shoulders; it is not a good look so perhaps discard it in favour of doing a random act of kindness and wear a smile. Don't wear someone else's personality. By all means learn from others, but be your own unique person.

CHAPTER TEN

It's about being positive

*Plan for the golden years - you may get
to experience them.*

Don't get to the end of your life just living the length of it, live the width of it as well, and do it with all your heart and soul (Diane Ackeridge). Life really is too short to sweat the small stuff. Dream big and enlarge the borders of your imagination.

As I discovered on the Camino, there were no short cuts, bar cheating. I learned that falling in the mud didn't spell the end of an adventure but rather initiated the beginning of the next stage of swallowing my pride, dumping my ego and taking care of my hip.

The chasm between your dreams and making them into a reality may seem vast, but perseverance, patience and backbone form part of the reward on your way to success.

Start at the beginning by holding your dream sharply in focus then follow through with action. Of this one thing you can be sure, if you don't take a step of action the only outcome can be disappointment. Without a breath of action your dream can never succeed but will remain as illusory as the proverbial pot of gold at the end of a rainbow.

So take that first step, if not today or this week, at least set a time of your own choosing. Each new day allow yourself to imagine rolling up your sleeves, then pulling on your socks, pushing back the boundaries of the things you thought possible, and discover fresh horizons, at first perhaps just a glimpse before realising your full potential.

In my early 50s, an idea that crept into my mind was to learn to ride a horse – quite a foolish idea you might think for someone who wouldn't even go near a field if a horse was there. Nonetheless came the day when I found myself, drenched in sweat and anxiety, sitting on a pony and, oh my goodness, the ground seemed a long way off. Then, to my dismay, the pony moved, just one foot, and nervousness almost paralysed my vocal chords as I squeaked to the riding instructor, 'What is it doing? Tell it to stop.' Exasperated, the instructor replied, 'It's moving one foot and then the next, that is what horses have to do to move forward.' I had a choice: to either feel the fear and do it anyway or get off and never learn to ride a horse. Sensibly I stayed put. You will, of course, understand that I never made the Olympic team but I did go on a pony riding holiday in Northumbria. That was achieved by continually reminding myself it was my goal in spite of falling off twice while still at the indoor riding school. On my first day out trekking my pony bolted while I clung on and screamed.

Life is too short to live it small. If you hit a brick wall of discouragement take note that the brick wall is there as an opportunity for you to pick yourself up, reappraise the situation, put your determination shoes on and then get moving. It is your own special character that will not allow you to devalue your dreams. It is your mindset alone that can shape your present and your future; it is your responsibility to choose how to follow your dream.

Your imagination can soar like a helium-filled balloon that tries to reach the sky; it might just reach above the treetops, but what a ride it had to get there.

While at university as a mature, getting on for ancient, student, my goal was a first-class degree and even the tutor's comments on my first assignment were not a deterrent as I read 'This is not an essay, it is a suet pudding with too many currants unevenly mixed.' I never did get a first-class degree but I had aimed high and got a second-class degree with honours. If my goal had been set lower the results might have been failure, but I shot for the moon and got the stars.

There is an Arabic proverb: Throw your heart out in front of you and run ahead to catch it.

CHAPTER ELEVEN

Role models and risk taking

As you pursue the reality of living your dreams allow yourself to do some risk taking. Don't avoid the challenges that are sure to arise and then find yourself in a comfortable niche that, horror of horrors, takes you to the end of your life wishing that you had allowed yourself to live.

Taking a look at some role models might be some incentive for you. Consider the well-known TV personality Carol Vorderman. She came to fame as a result of her role on the TV programme *Countdown* but currently she is on the countdown to an astonishing adventure. At the time of writing, she is 56; however, in her early 50s she took flying lessons with the aim that, one day, she would fly solo around the world. Her dream is excitingly nearing reality. Although she had long dreamed of this venture she kept putting it off as her friends and family thought it was foolish or impossible. Why? Because she was considered too old. But now Carol is on the verge of an exhilarating hybrid of personal journey and extreme challenge. She has shown that it is not too late to fulfil your dream if you just have the gumption to make the effort. That solo voyage might not happen but what a ride Carol has had preparing herself for the possibility.

You may be tremendously relieved that flying solo around the world is not on your horizon, but dust down your own dream – perhaps to study, to write poetry, to play the guitar, to learn a language or line dancing. Whatever your choice, honour yourself with the dignity of living while you are alive. I have a 60-year-old friend determined to join in with her husband's love of motorbike riding. On the first day, she sat on the pillion seat, fell off and broke her arm – and the bike hadn't yet moved! But she knew where she was heading and wasn't going to let a plastered arm be a deterrent.

Lady Margaret Tebbit, wife of the politician Sir Norman Tebbit, after being caught up in the catastrophic bombing of the Brighton Grand Hotel, was paralysed from the neck down and confined to a wheelchair. Five people were killed as the Tory Party Conference was being held. Lady Margaret's husband and the then Prime Minister, Margaret Thatcher, were rescued. Margaret's spine was crushed as she fell through four floors of the wrecked building. Refusing to dwell on the past, this stalwart of a woman had new priorities and she has a dream which she manages to put into reality. No flying solo round the world for her, it was simply to go shopping on her own to choose her own clothes, and she does. Guiding her electric wheelchair with the sole use of just one thumb, which is kept strengthened with intensive physiotherapy, she takes herself to the major stores and small boutiques. She values her independence highly.

So, consider, does the thumb of your dreams have some movement?

Today is the only day you have; a current buzzword is 'mindfulness' which simply means living in the present. Whether you are eating pizza and chips or spending time with a friend, enjoy the moment; relish the delicious mozzarella snaking off your fork, enjoy the cheese meting into succulent ham. If you are out with a friend, pay attention, this moment will never come back again, so listen, notice such things as the colour of nail varnish or a new hairstyle. Notice yourself, enjoy the chair you are sitting on, even the gateau you have made for your family's evening meal.

Living with a sense of awareness rather than drifting aimlessly can be aligned to the concept of giving, and giving a smile is a good place to start.

Recently I read of a woman who, at the age of 60 plus, with her children now independent adults, and having reasonable health and her work pension intact, realised that she could do some incredible things if she disregarded the barriers and conventions imposed by society. An impulse trip to Asia with her son challenged her to sell her small business and to travel, working overseas wherever possible to supplement her income.

This amazingly motivated woman has 'casually' wandered around Asia, Europe, America and Australia. Casual is the word she uses to describe her travels. Living frugally but safely, her pension is sufficient to get by while staying in hostels, travelling by bus and eating like the locals. Her main expense has been air fares. This lady has no hankering for air conditioning, soft fluffy towels or the isolation of a hotel room. Her fellow travellers are an eclectic mix including gap year students, midlifers, families, and even grandparents. Packing light, taking only what she could carry, her nomadic lifestyle is combined with overseas voluntary work. This is a lady who stopped dreaming her life and lived her dream.

Maybe you are not feeling so intrepid but would still like to travel and to make a difference out there in the world. VSO, Voluntary Service Overseas, might be your answer.

VSO looks for experienced professional people who would like to find out more about opportunities to work overseas; if you fit into this category then this could well be just the choice for you. VSO has placements for you to use your skills and experiences in a way that will have a long-lasting impact on the lives of disadvantaged people as you bring inspiration, energy, and of course your skills to help secure better healthcare, education and utilities for poor people in Africa or Asia. For more information visit: **enquiry@vsoint.org**

All your travel, vaccinations, expenses and accommodation are paid for, and this includes comprehensive training. You share your time and expertise, not your money.

So, if you have at least three years' experience in your speciality, have a degree or relevant qualification, you are fit and healthy, can pass the DBS check (formerly known as CRB), and you are willing to commit to the whole of your placement and you are willing to adapt, this could be just the opportunity for you in your retirement to do something with your itchy feet and accumulated knowledge. Placements can be from six months to two years.

VSO needs various skills including medical, educational, market and skills analysis, finance, vocational training including fishery and farming, and vehicle maintenance among others.

Let's talk about other ways to enable you to better enjoy your third age years and beyond when you don't have pots of money or don't want to go anywhere near a gym. Here is a gentle starter. Sir Richard Stilgoe, singer and songwriter, is quoted as providing some useful exercises for the face. Look up not down. Look forward not back. Raise the side of your mouth – in other words – smile.

Meanwhile, there is so much encouragement out there for you to get fit. TV carries advertisements for healthy eating and healthy living. Leaflets for the latest local gym drop through your letterbox. Magazines of all kinds seem to find a slot to beckon you towards a fitter lifestyle, but inwardly you groan as you think of the cost, time and effort. And cost is a big issue for many people. So the top tip for today is that you can be your own gym instructor.

If you walk reasonably fast for just half an hour each day you have made a good start. You might not even have noticed that half-hour walk to the shops, or while exercising the dog. Try getting off the bus a bus stop early; there is no cost involved and you are on the first rung of your exercise programme.

If being competitive suits you, by all means go for it, but basically just enjoy the activity and the blessing of being able to do whatever the venture you have chosen.

Here are some suggestions that might cost some money, but when viewed as an evening out, or a social activity, the cost is already absorbed. How about swimming or aquarobics? You might prefer socialising while enjoying the rhythm of dancing: ballroom, line dancing, Zumba or jive. Whatever your choice of activity, just be sure to do it regularly. You will most likely find it helpful to do something that can be incorporated into the routine of your daily or social life.

To help you to maintain a good balance, posture and to relieve the tedium of backache, how about joining a Pilates or yoga class? A few years ago I did Tai Chi for a while and found it very beneficial. However, when I enquired about kick-boxing the class supervisor ruled me out on age. On reminding him that these days we don't do ageism, the poor young man, backed into a corner, thought for a moment then decided there wouldn't be anyone of my age to pair me up with. Clever thinking on his part, but it was not at all helpful for my ambitions.

CHAPTER TWELVE

Wrapping up the Camino Experience

It is important to stay fit and healthy as you age; this is so you can remain as independent and happy as possible as you grow older. Staying fit is about more than exercise, it keeps your mind active along with other pursuits like reading, music, staying ahead of current events.

When embarking on my Camino adventure, although I had done the extra preparatory walking, I took a sensible look at my diet and worked towards general fitness. I wasn't at all athletic, but that wasn't what it was about nor is it necessarily so for you. It isn't about being athletic but about being fit. Did you know that if you did no exercise after the age of 50 you will lose around 550g of muscle a year, and if you are unfit and over the age of 70, there is an 80% increased risk of diabetes and heart problems.

Australian researchers suggest that taking up exercise at any age is worthwhile for both mind and body. They suggest that thinking and memory skills are much improved when people exercise both the heart and the muscle regularly, even for those who are showing signs of cognitive decline.

You might wonder if it really is worth all the bother, after all you might not even get old! On the other hand, you just might and this is just a little present you are giving to your future self. Somebody, somewhere, and I don't remember who, has said that you are preparing the person of today to be the person of the future, of your own tomorrow.

Getting physical is about more than your bones and muscles, it is also essential for good mental health as you get older. Remember it remains true that it is rarely too late to become the person you might have been if you had started earlier.

Of course, you may be reading this and wishing all of the above were a possibility but, because you are unable to get out of a chair, especially a wheelchair, exercise just isn't going to happen and adaptability becomes the name of the game. I am currently reading an easy to read, well-illustrated book, *Sod Sitting, Get Moving* by Diana Moran and Muir Gray. I recommend it for whatever your level of enthusiasm or ability may be.

Don't let your age, your height or your width be a hindrance.

The book *Sod Sitting, Get Moving* contains an excellent guide to exercising from a wheelchair, so get moving and boost your level of endorphins to make a happy and healthier you. For sure, getting older remains inevitable but getting fitter is optional. Getting older isn't for wimps; it takes courage to handle diminishing prowess and encroaching frailty. If there are areas where you can take a measure of control to thwart those potential difficulties then it is wise to do so. Again, your older self will thank your younger self for such forethought.

Don't underestimate yourself, you are built for growth not for stagnation. You are built to discover ways to fulfil a deep-felt need to give back to society and, in doing so, to quietly build your own markers. Remember that every day above ground is a good one and every new morning is a gift, a fresh opportunity.

For the moment you may be a third ager but unfortunately this too will pass, so it is a good time to start thinking of ways in which you can bless the person you are going to become.

I have already written of the way in which my Camino adventure echoed life. Life has diverse moments, some of them terribly sad or difficult, many of them incredibly enriching and beautiful. My Camino neared its end as we entered the ancient Santiago square with its imposing cathedral. My daughter and I punched the air and jumped as high as our backpacks would allow with the utter exuberance of accomplishment. Then we entered the cathedral itself. This was a moment of stillness and joy as we joined hundreds of others sitting in the coolness of the building to be still and to reflect that in spite of the mud and the heat we did it. Not that we thought this was the end, but rather it was the onward process of thinking, if I could do this, then what else can I do?

But in that moment of stillness there was another, deeper reflection. Along the way we had walked alongside other peregrinos (pilgrims) and in that rarefied atmosphere far away from the details of home life, people would share their stories. People had hiked their Caminos for various reasons, but usually the stories they told were of pain and of loss. On arrival in Santiago and entering the cathedral for the midday Pilgrim's Mass, a whole new meaning was perceived in the sharing of the Eucharist, which you may have heard of as called Communion, the Sacrament, or Breaking of Bread, and which is a sacred moment during a church service acknowledging the sacrificial love of God for humanity through his son Jesus Christ. Also experienced differently was the Passing the Peace of Christ, a feature of many church services; in practice, the congregation usually shake hands with each other while saying, 'The peace of Christ to you.' In essence it means each person is wanting to share with the others something of their experience of faith in Christ, almost as if offering the peace as a gift. To be honoured with these rituals among people who we met on the journey, whose stories of pain, loss and bewilderment had been shared as they walked, these things gave a very different emphasis to the traditional theology. It is unlikely that I shall ever sit comfortably on a church pew again without remembering the depth of what the unity of sharing our faith really can mean.

A totally awesome cathedral experience was the swinging of the Botafumeiro; this huge brass incense burner was skilfully swung by several priests who, working together, pulled on ropes to make it swing both high and around the cathedral. For those of us sitting in the long rows facing the altar, to have this huge container swing almost past our shoulders before arching its way above the naves was a never to be forgotten experience, and one that contained so much imagery. For me, the incense hovering all around us before wafting its way higher and higher to the upper reaches spoke poignantly of prayer and gave a whole new meaning to passing the peace with people from many nations and with many complicated sorrows.

I looked around me and saw the fine young Italian man who, having lost his faith in God, was challenged by his priest to go on the Camino – taking nothing at all with him, not even money. 'D' told us his story, how he had found God to be real in the lives of the people he had met on his pilgrimage. On the further aisle, sitting huddled up with her grief was a young German woman whose husband had walked out. I hugged the American man who, finding the pilgrimage too tough, had wanted to quit, but there he was standing tall and so pleased to have completed his challenge. It seemed that the rising incense echoed the holiness of prayer as it wrapped itself around all these people, taking up their sadness and their joys to hold in the presence of the living God. This was something that made the pilgrimage complete.

I came home exhilarated, shattered, slimmer and very proud of my amazing daughter who enabled my pilgrimage on this extraordinary Camino journey.

You may not be able to, or wish to, go hiking the Camino, nor may you wish to go to university. Your third age years cannot be replicated in anyone else's life because you alone are you and living in your own set of circumstances. But within your own parameters carve out for yourself that amazing thing called living; as far as possible live your dreams.

Whatever your adventure or choice will be, I wish you well.

Best wishes

Angela

CHAPTER THIRTEEN

Helpful information

www.FutureLearn.com
A free OU resource to explore ageing

Voluntary Service Overseas (VSO)
www.vsointernational.org
For volunteering overseas

Acorn Listening courses
01420 478121

University of the Third Age
020 8466 6139

BELOW – *part of my later life story*

Here are some tongue in cheek ideas to think about!

Things old people say – and don't say them – start practising now:

1. Someone heaving out of a chair –
   'Don't get old dear.'

2. Young people – the clothes they wear or almost don't wear – just get used to it and don't say,
   'It wasn't like that in my day.'

3. It's not acceptable to say, 'When I was young...' until you are at least 100; at that point it might be interesting, before that is boring.

4. 'Excuse my poor voice, I rarely see anyone these days so don't get the chance to talk.' Oooops, guilt.

5. On the same line, 'Nobody comes near or by, no one wants to know you when you are old.' There might be some truth in that, on the other hand interesting/interested (and praying) older people are lovely to be around, particularly if they show genuine uncritical interest.

6. When tempted to criticise young people remember they haven't yet had the opportunity to know what it is like to be older – but age has the benefit of hindsight and knows what it is like to be young and how awful it was to be criticised.

About the author

Angela Susannah Lucas now aged 83 (2017) spent her wartime childhood years in Rhyl, north Wales. This was a time of learning self-sufficiency and contributing to the family larder by mushrooming, blackberry picking and setting fishing night lines at the receding tide to catch a good supply of plaice for her family and neighbours.

Alongside marriage and the birth of her five children, 'her main accomplishment', she followed a career in nursing. In her 50s redundancy encouraged a change in career, prompting study for the Private Secretary's Certificate. This led to work in Saudi Arabia as a medical secretary and later as a TEFL teacher in Egypt teaching English while attempting to learn basic Arabic.

Retirement gave opportunity for further study, first for A Level English, followed by university and three consecutive degrees. To celebrate her 82nd birthday the author hiked the final 100 kilometres (62 miles) of the ancient Camino de Santiago in the Galician mountains of northern Spain.

Studies behind her and drawing on her own experiences, Angela has just completed her first book, a motivational read to encourage living a life full of purpose for those in their 50s, 60s and beyond.

Printed in Great Britain
by Amazon